The Look-it-up Book of
Birds

The Look-it-u

Book of **Birds**

By Elizabeth S. Austin and Oliver L. Austin
Revised by Neil Ardley

Illustrated by Richard E. Amundsen
and George Thompson

Collins · GLASGOW AND LONDON

We are most grateful to Dr Mary Heimerdinger Clench, Associate Curator of
Birds at the Carnegie Museum of Pittsburgh, Pennsylvania, for her careful reading
of the original manuscript and her helpful suggestions. Dr Pierce Brodkorb of the
faculty of the University of Florida and Dr E. G. Franz Sauer, Director of the
Natural History Museum, University of Bonn, Germany, have been most generous
with information and we thank them sincerely. We also appreciate the cooperation
of the staff of the University of Florida Research Library.

First published in this edition 1973
Published by William Collins Sons and Company Limited, Glasgow and London
© 1970 by Random House, Inc. All rights reserved under International and
Pan-American Copyright Conventions.
© 1973 additional text and drawings William Collins Sons and Company Limited

Printed in Great Britain
ISBN 0 00 102205 9

Introduction

Many people find birds the most captivating and interesting of all animals. It is not difficult to see why. Birds not only fly, which is a most enviable ability, but they also have good eyesight and can see in colour. This means that they often dress in bright colours and bold patterns, in contrast with most other animals which have a drab, dull appearance. Birds have fascinating ways of breeding and their courtship, nests and eggs are of great interest.

The study of birds is not difficult; all you have to do is open your eyes and keep quiet. Birds can be seen everywhere and there are enough of them to make bird watching a life-long hobby. Whether observing birds at a bird box or bird table in the garden or making special expeditions to remote areas rich in bird interest, the behaviour and beauty of birds always rewards awareness. Bird ringing is a way in which bird study can be carried out scientifically with greater accuracy. Finding and reporting the discovery of a ringed bird not only tells us where it travels, but also how long it lives in the wild. Much of what this book tells about birds comes from the discoveries of bird watchers and bird ringers, both professional and amateur.

There are more than 8600 different species of birds and they are grouped into about 160 families. All the birds in a family have bodies that are built in the same way internally, even though they may look very different on the outside. Some families are very large; the family of flycatchers, thrushes, babblers and warblers contains about 1200 species. Other families are small and some, such as the secretary bird and the hoatzin, contain only one species. Families are grouped together into orders, and more than half of all the species of birds belong to one order – that of the perching birds. Each entry in this book usually deals with birds of one family. In the illustrations, the sex of a bird is shown by the symbols all scientists use. These are the signs that astronomers use for planets. The mirror of Venus ♀ indicates female and the arrow of Mars ♂ male. When no sign is used, the male and female birds are alike.

Albatrosses

Laysan albatross

Black-footed albatross

The albatrosses, of which there are 13 different kinds, are the world's largest sea birds. The wandering albatross is the largest albatross and it has the greatest wingspan of any bird – 11½ feet (340 centimetres). Albatrosses spend most of their lives soaring with the winds over the oceans, flying for hours with hardly a movement of their wings. They do this by repeatedly soaring up into the wind with their wings outstretched and then turning and zooming down towards the waves with their wings bent into a W shape to gain speed. At the last moment, they skim over the waves, stretch their wings and soar back into the sky. For hundreds of years, sailors have watched albatrosses following their ships, seeking fish or squid in the ship's wake or scraps thrown overboard. As these birds need wind to fly, superstitious seamen thought that albatrosses brought the wind with them.

Without a wind, an albatross is almost helpless. It has to rest on the water until the wind blows again. For this reason, albatrosses are unable to cross the doldrums, the region of calm weather at the equator. So the ten species of albatross that live in the southern seas are very rarely seen in the northern hemisphere. However, three separate species of albatrosses do live in the North Pacific Ocean. These three northern albatrosses are the laysan albatross, the black-footed albatross and the short-tailed albatross.

The wandering albatross is the best-known of the ten southern albatrosses. It is four feet (120 centimetres) long from the tip of its tail to the end of its bill but it weighs only about 25 pounds (11 kilograms). Its wings stretch to the record span of 11½ feet (340 centimetres). The royal albatross is slightly smaller with a wingspan of nine feet (270 centimetres). Even the smallest albatrosses have a wingspan of six feet (180 centimetres) or more. Albatrosses are black and white in colour, or greyish brown all over. The wandering albatross resembles the laysan albatross, except that its underside is completely white apart from its black wingtips.

Albatrosses spend most of their time roaming the southern seas around Antartica, where the 'roaring forties' and other winds blow and the seas are rich in food. They may cover as much as 250 miles (400 kilometres) in a day and so can circle the world in as little as 80 days at these latitudes. Albatrosses nest on remote ocean islands. The smaller species return to their nesting grounds every October to December, when it is warm in the southern seas. It is thought that wandering albatrosses nest every other year.

Albatrosses lay a single egg that takes two months or more to hatch. It is then another three to six months before the young albatross is ready to fly, and a further two or three months before it leaves the nest. The young albatross must then spend the next six years or so wandering about the oceans learning to fend for itself, before it is old enough to breed and can return to the nesting grounds.

Antbirds

Chestnut-backed antbird

The antbirds are a family of 223 species of dull-coloured birds that live in South and Central America. They live low in jungle trees or on the ground amid the undergrowth where they can be near the ants on which they depend for food. Some species of antbirds follow columns of marching ants, eating not only the insects but also the small creatures that flee at the approach of the foraging army.

Antbirds are from four to 14 inches (ten to 35 centimetres) in length, and are mostly brownish black in colour. They have various names all beginning with *ant* followed by another bird's name, such as antwren, antshrike, antvireo, and antpitta. Of course they all resemble the bird that makes up the second half of their name in some way. The antwren is a small bird, like the wren, and the antvireo builds nests in a similar way to the vireo.

Spotted antbird

Auks

The auks are a family of 22 species of seabirds. They spend most of their lives at sea, only coming ashore to breed on the cliffs of rocky coasts and islands. Auks live in the cold Arctic Ocean and neighbouring seas and oceans. Six species of auks live in the North Atlantic and breed around the coasts of Britain, Iceland and Scandinavia. They are the razorbill, the common guillemot or common murre, and Brunnich's guillemot, which are all 16 inches (40 centimetres) long, the little auk or dovekie, which is eight inches (20 centimetres) in length, and the black guillemot and the puffin, which are both about 12 inches (30 centimetres) long.

Like penguins, auks are chunky birds and excellent swimmers. They dive down from the surface of the sea and pursue fish underwater by 'rowing' with their wings and steering with their feet. However, unlike penguins, they are good fliers.

Auks are black and white birds which change their plumage twice a year. The black guillemot, which is black all over except for a white wing patch, becomes almost completely white in winter. The common puffin alters little in plumage, but its face changes with the season. In summer its face is white and its strange parrot-like bill is a gaudy red and yellow. But in winter its face darkens and the colours of the bill become dull. The puffin's bill becomes brighter in the spring as the breeding season approaches, and several auks grow courting plumes, crests or other special markings at this time. But the crested auklet, of the Bering Sea and North Pacific coasts, always bears a crest.

Auks do their hunting at sea in silence but, with the exception of puffins, they make up for this when they come ashore to nest. Then thousands of birds gather in huge and noisy auk colonies completely covering cliffs and rocks by the sea. The birds often return to the same ledge to breed every year. They fly to high cliffs

Great auk with egg (extinct

Black guillemot (winter plumage)

facing the sea, and each pair of birds incubates a single egg. They raise their chick crowded wing to wing with other pairs along the narrow ledges. The eggs are pear-shaped. This is helpful, because if an egg is touched, it just rolls around the pointed end instead of rolling off the ledge and smashing on a rock below. In some species, the chicks flutter down to the water only two weeks after they hatch and start to swim with their parents. Chicks of other species wait until they can swim unaided before leaving the nest.

Common puffins have a different way of breeding. They dig a short burrow in grassy slopes on the cliffs near the sea, or use an old rabbit burrow. The young puffin hatches and is raised in the burrow. The black guillemot, which is the only auk to lay two eggs, and the little auk nest on cliffs. They hide their eggs and chicks in nooks and crannies among the rocks.

The twenty-third member of the auk family lives now only in history and legend. The great auk, which was 30 inches (76 centimetres) long and could not fly, once bred on islands in the North Atlantic Ocean near the Arctic Circle. But it could not easily defend itself or escape by flying away. Hunters killed the great auks for their meat, oil and feathers. The last great auks were killed on an islet off Iceland on 3rd June 1844.

Common guillemot

Crested auklet

Little auk

Common puffin

Avocets

Avocet

Avocets and stilts are seven species of elegant wading birds from 15 to 18 inches (38 to 46 centimetres) in size. They are easy to tell apart: avocets have long bills that curve gently upwards and stilts have straight bills. Also, the stilt has pink legs. Avocets and stilts live in shallow bays or lagoons, marshes and ponds, probing the bottom with their long bills for food.

Avocets and stilts are found in most parts of the world. The avocet of Europe, Asia and Africa is black and white, but the American avocet and the red-necked avocet of Australia both have a reddish brown head and neck. Stilts usually have white bellies and black backs, but there are some all-black stilts in New Zealand and the banded stilt of Australia has an orange-brown band across its chest. The black-winged stilt lives in warm regions around the world.

Babblers

Striped jungle babbler

Babblers are a family of nearly 300 species of widely differing birds. They get their name from their chattering voices. Babblers live in woods, mostly in Africa, Asia and Australasia. Few babblers are found in Europe and only one occurs in America. Babblers range in size from small tit-like birds to birds the size of small crows. The bearded tit, which is found in parts of Europe as well as throughout Asia, is six and a half inches (16 centimetres) long. It has a moustache of black stripes. The striped jungle babbler of the forests of south-east Asia is the same size. It is difficult to spot among the foliage.

One of the most interesting babblers is the logrunner of Australia. This is the only bird which is known to use its tail and feet to rake the ground for insects and other creatures. The largest group of babblers is that of the laughing thrushes of Africa, India and south-east Asia. The noise of chattering groups of laughing thrushes sounds rather like people laughing. These birds are from four to 12 inches (ten to 30 centimetres) in length.

One of the largest and strangest babblers is the bare-headed rock fowl or bald crow, of which there are two species. They live on high ground in West Africa, and are 14 inches (35 centimetres) long. The head of this bird has no feathers, and so looks very small in comparison with the size of its body.

Bee-eaters

The European bee-eater is the most colourful bird to be found in Europe. It has a blue breast, yellow throat, reddish brown back and red and green wings. Bee-eaters live in open country, and can be seen perching on colourful flocks on wires or branches. They live in southern Europe in the summer, and spend the winter in Africa. The European bee-eater is 11 inches (27 centimetres) long. It is one of 24 species of bee-eaters, and the others live in the warm parts of Asia, Africa and Australasia. In Australia, bee-eaters are known as rainbow birds. One of the most striking bee-eaters is the carmine bee-eater of central Africa. It has a bright crimson body and turquoise blue head.

Bee-eaters get their name from their habit of eating bees, which they take on the wing in short, swift flights. Like kingfishers, to which they are related, bee-eaters lay their eggs in burrows which they tunnel into banks.

Carmine bee-eater

European bee-eater

Birds of Paradise

The birds of paradise have long been famous for their beautiful appearance. Their colourful sprays of feathers and long delicate plumes have been admired by people for centuries. Nobody knows for sure when the first bird of paradise feathers came to Europe. But the *Victoria*, the only ship to survive the first round-the-world expedition, came home to Spain in 1522 with two bird of paradise skins. They were a gift from the ruler of Batjan, one of the Moluccas or Spice Islands. The Spaniards were so struck by the bird's beauty that they believed it could come only from paradise, and the birds have been known as birds of paradise ever since.

It is only the male birds of paradise that have such wonderful plumage. The females are dull and drab in appearance. The males display their fine feathers in elaborate courtship dances to attract the females. The blue bird of paradise hangs upside-down from a branch, waving its misty blue feathers. The magnificent bird of paradise clears itself an 'arena' in the forest in which to perform for its mate. It is thought that birds of paradise have such extraordinary displays in order that the female can easily recognize a male of her own species.

But, although she has been courted so beautifully, the female bird of paradise usually gets no help in raising the young after mating. She has to build the nest herself, and feed and care for the pair of chicks that hatch from the two brown-streaked orange eggs.

There are 42 different species of birds of paradise. Thirty six are in New Guinea and neighbouring islands, and four are found in north-eastern Australia. The most beautiful are the birds of the genus *Paradisaea*, with their long sprays of feathers. These birds include the red-plumed bird of paradise, which measures 18 inches (46 centimetres) in length. The king bird of paradise and the magnificent bird of paradise are smaller birds with elongated tail plumes. The king bird of paradise is the smallest member of the family, having a length of six inches (15 centimetres), and it is the only bird of paradise to nest in a hole in a tree. Another group of birds of paradise is made up of the flag birds, which have plumes growing from the head. The King of Saxony bird of paradise is a flag bird. In spite of their appearance, birds of paradise are distantly related to crows and, like crows, they are noisy birds. Some birds of paradise are called riflebirds, because their whistling call is rather like the whine of a bullet. The magnificent riflebird has a handsome iridescent purple-blue throat. It poses with its wings spread and head thrown back to show off its throat.

The names of some birds of paradise are preceded with royal names, such as Queen Victoria's riflebird and Prince Rudolph's blue bird of paradise. This is because the naturalists who first discovered these birds of paradise named them after the rulers of their countries at that time.

The plumes of birds of paradise were once used for ladies' hats, capes and fans. The species that could be sold for the highest prices came close to extinction. Among these were several beautiful birds, including the lesser bird of paradise, the Emperor of Germany's bird of paradise, and the greater bird of paradise. Happily, strict laws passed in 1924 saved these birds from the ravages of fashion.

King of Saxony
bird of paradise

♂

King bird of paradise
♂

♂
Red-plumed bird of paradise

Prince Rudolph's
♂ blue bird of paradise

♂

Magnificent bird of paradise

Blackbirds

See Thrushes

Boobies

See Gannets

Bowerbirds

♂   **Golden bowerbird**

The males of the 18 species of bowerbirds of New Guinea and northern Australia do not possess the marvellous courting plumes of their neighbours, the birds of paradise. But they excel at courting in a different way. All but two of the bowerbirds clear a space in the undergrowth and make special arenas in which they stage their courting displays. The bowerbirds known as maypole builders build a roofed structure like a hut by interweaving twigs in the way that nests are made. The hut is constructed around a tree trunk that acts as a central pole. The male also decorates the courting ground outside the hut with leaves, flowers, berries, shells, fruit, feathers and other bright objects. The golden bowerbird of Australia is only 12 inches (30 centimetres) long, but it builds a hut as high as nine feet (270 centimetres)! To 19th-century explorers in Australia,

the huts looked like summer houses – then called 'bowers' – and this is how the bowerbirds came to be named.

Another group of bowerbirds is the avenue builders. Their bowers consist of walled passageways, sometimes partly roofed. The floor of the avenue may be matted, and the bower is decorated with flowers, feathers and other objects. The satin bowerbird and regent bowerbird, both about 12 inches (30 centimetres) long, decorate their bowers with a blue or green paint made by mixing charcoal and other pigments with saliva or fruit pulp. The birds use a wad of leaves or pieces of shredded bark to paint. This is a rare example of a bird using a tool. A third group of bowerbirds, the stage makers, simply clear a space three to five feet (90 to 150 centimetres) across and lay down fresh leaves to decorate the courting ground.

Once their bowers are complete, the male bowerbirds lure the females by singing loudly and clearly from a perch near or inside the bower. The males also perform special courting dances, and the females come to the bowers to watch.

After mating, the female goes off to build a cup-shaped nest high in a tree. She lays two eggs, incubates them and raises her young without any help from the male. He continues to sing and pose in his bower.

Budgerigars

See Parrots

Buntings

Bunting is a name given to several different kinds of seed-eating birds. In the New World, buntings are colourful birds, especially the vivid painted bunting. In the Old World, buntings are mostly greyish brown birds from five to seven inches (13 to 18 centimetres) long. Buntings have short, thick bills that enable them to crack open seeds, and they live in open country. The corn bunting is a very common bunting in Europe. It is streaked grey-brown. The yellowhammer or yellow bunting is easier to spot, with its bright yellow breast and head. The reed bunting lives among reed beds, and in the summer the male can easily be identified by its black hood and bib and white collar. The snow bunting breeds in Arctic regions around the world. It is a winter visitor to Europe, Asia, and North America.

Painted bunting
♀

Lark bunting
♂

*Snow bunting
(winter plumage)*

Bustards

Bustards are a family of 22 greyish brown birds that live throughout the Old World except in northern Europe and northern Asia. They are large birds, and the giant bustard of southern Africa is probably the largest bird that can fly. It is 54 inches (137 centimetres) long and weighs up to 50 pounds (23 kilograms). The great bustard, which is slightly smaller, is the largest bird found in Europe.

Bustards roam grasslands and, although they can fly, they usually escape their enemies by running or trying to hide. They are an easy target for hunters, and bustards have to be protected by law.

♂
Great bustard

Buzzards

Buzzard is a name given to several different kinds of birds of prey, but a true buzzard belongs to the genus *Buteo*. This genus contains about 26 species of large hawks. The common buzzard is a large dark brown bird with a wingspan of four feet (120 centimetres) and a grey hooked beak. It feeds on small animals such as rats, rabbits, birds, reptiles and fish. Common buzzards breed in Europe and central Asia and migrate south in winter. The honey buzzard is a bird of a separate family that attacks the nests of bees and wasps. It eats the insects themselves and not their honey.

Common buzzard

Canaries

Canaries are very popular as cage birds. They are finches, and wild canary finches live in the Canary Islands. These are brown-flecked olive green birds with yellowish green breasts, and they do not sing well. Sailors first brought wild canaries to Europe four centuries ago, and people bred them and crossed them with other finches so that they soon developed the yellow plumage and trilling song that we enjoy so much today.

Canary

Cardinals

A Roman Catholic cardinal wears robes of a glowing red colour, and so cardinal is a very good name for this common red bird of North America. It is eight inches (20 centimetres) long and has a crest on its head. Cardinals like to live in cities and towns. They do not usually move south for the winter, and the red flash of a cardinal against the white winter snow is a thrilling sight.

♂ *Cardinal*

Chaffinches

The chaffinch is perhaps the prettiest common bird to be found in Britain and western Europe. It is so common that there are thought to be about ten million chaffinches in Britain. Chaffinches are found throughout Europe, and in Asia and northern Africa. The total world population must be some 200 million. The chaffinch is six inches (15 centimetres) long, and the male has a pink breast, a blue top to its head, and a reddish brown and green back. It has a double white bar on its wings and a white-edged tail. The female has the same markings, but is a greyish yellow colour.

Chaffinch ♂

21

Chickens

White Plymouth Rock

Longtailed Yokohama

Buff Orpington

Chickens are domestic birds, raised in thousands of millions for their eggs and meat. The domestic chicken is the most common bird on earth – in fact, there are more chickens on earth than people! There are many different varieties of domestic chickens, including the white Plymouth Rock and the buff Orpington. But they are all descended from a single wild species – the jungle fowl of India and south-east Asia. A few chickens are bred for their beautiful plumage. In Japan, the roosters of the longtailed Yokohama are raised for their beautiful trailing tails, which may grow to a length of 20 feet (six metres). In some countries, cocks are bred for their fighting qualities and these are the chickens which most resemble their wild ancestors. Cock fighting is against the law in many countries.

Cockatoos

See Parrots

Cocks of the rock

The cock of the rock is a bird with a strange appearance to complement its strange name. It has a huge crest of feathers on the front of its head which makes the eyes seem to be set very far back. The crest sometimes falls over the bill, so that the bird appears to have no beak. At breeding time, cocks of the rock gather in groups and each male performs a hopping dance before the females. Cocks of the rock live in South America. There are two species: the males of one species are orange, and the males of the other are bright red. The females of both species are light brown.

Golden cock of the rock

♂

Great cormorant

Cormorants

These web-footed water birds are at home in large lakes and rivers as well as the sea coasts of the world. They never go far from land. The smallest of the 30 species is the pygmy cormorant, which is 18 inches (45 centimetres) long and lives in south-eastern Europe and Asia. The largest cormorant is the common cormorant or great cormorant, which is 40 inches (100 centimetres) in length. Cormorants are also called *shags*.

With the exception of the flightless cormorant of the Galapagos Islands, which does not fly at all, cormorants are strong fliers. They can be seen flying in formations or in groups. Cormorants are also strong swimmers. They feed by diving from the surface to chase fish underwater. Cormorants like small eels and slow-swimming fish such as cod and carp.

After he has caught a fish, the cormorant swims with it to the surface of the water. The bird tosses the fish into the air or twists it about in its beak so that the fish can be swallowed head first. After some time in the water, the bird comes ashore or perches on a rock or buoy and spreads its wings to dry them.

In China and Japan, fishermen make use of the skill of the great cormorant by training teams of birds to fish for them. They take the cormorants out at dusk in their boats. Each bird is attached to a leash and has a ring around its neck. This ring prevents the cormorant from swallowing any large fish that it catches. It returns to its owner with its bill full of large fish, which it gives up to the fisherman. Cormorants are also useful to man for their droppings, or *guano*, which is a valuable fertilizer.

Cormorants breed in colonies. They build bulky nests on the ground or in trees. There are usually two to four eggs and both parents sit on them. The young are born naked and blind and are fed by the parents on half-digested food.

Cowbirds

Brown-headed cowbird

Cowbirds are the main parasitic birds in the New World, as cuckoos are in the Old World. Parasitic birds lay their eggs in the nests of other birds. The other bird then raises the young intruder, who may push the bird's own eggs or young out of the nest. Some cowbirds will lay their eggs only in the nests of one particular bird. Other cowbirds, such as the brown-headed cowbird, lay in many kinds of nests. But some cowbirds such as the baywinged cowbird, rear their own young. But this bird also has to act as a host to the screaming cowbird, which lays its eggs only in the nests of baywinged cowbirds!

Cranes

These elegant birds, with their long legs and necks and stately bearing, are found throughout the world, with the exception of South America, New Zealand, Malaysia and the Pacific Islands. Cranes live in marshlands and plains. There are 15 species of cranes, most of which are in need of protection as their numbers are low. Cranes are long-lived birds, and are revered in the East as symbols of long life and happiness. But they are less fortunate elsewhere. In America, only a few whooping cranes exist after much hunting and many man-made changes in their wintering grounds.

The tall and stately sarus crane is the world's largest wading bird. It is five feet (150 centimetres) in length and lives in India and south-east Asia. Sarus cranes are very tame. Mated pairs sometimes become household pets and live in the garden, acting as watchdogs. The dainty demoiselle crane is the smallest crane, and is three feet (90 centimetres) long. It lives in the southern and central parts of Europe and Asia. It is a pretty bird, light grey in colour with white plumes

Sarus crane

Crowned crane

reaching from behind its eyes and down its neck. The crowned crane of Africa is slightly larger than the demoiselle crane and has a majestic crest of golden feathers.

Cranes perform elaborate group dances. Some species dance only during the breeding season, but others dance all through the year. The dance starts when two birds strut around each other with their wings half open. They bow to each other, stretch their necks and bills towards the sky, and then leap high in the air with feet gracefully pointed towards the ground – just like a pair of ballet dancers. As the dance continues, it becomes wilder and more cranes join in with croaks, whoops, honks and trumpeting sounds. All cranes have long, curling windpipes that produce their trumpeting calls. These calls are often heard before a flock of cranes takes to the air. The cranes fly in a great V-formation or in a long regular line.

Tree creeper

Creepers

Creepers are small birds found mostly in the Old World. The tree creeper is easily recognized. It is five inches (13 centimetres) long, is brown with white underparts, and has a slender, down-curving beak. It can be seen probing tree trunks for insects. Tree creepers live in forests throughout Europe, Asia and North America. In Australia, tree creepers are similar birds that also feed on the ground. The wallcreeper, which inhabits mountains in Europe and Asia, climbs rocky cliffs in search of food. The wallcreeper has bright red and black wings with white spots.

Demoiselle crane

Crossbills

Crossbills get their name from their unusual sharp-edged beak, the tips of which cross over like a pair of crossed fingers. They also have very strong jaw muscles, so that they can easily cut through the outer scales of cones to get at the seeds inside.

Crossbills are finches and they live in pine forests and other coniferous woodlands. They are nomadic birds, wandering from place to place in search of food. The common crossbill is found in North America, Europe and Asia. It is red with dark wings and tail, and is known as the red crossbill in America. The white-winged crossbill is a similar bird, except that it has white markings on its wings.

Crossbills raise four young a year. Soon after they fledge, their bills lengthen and become crossed.

Common crossbill
♂

White-winged crossbill
♂

Crows

Rooks, jackdaws, ravens, magpies, jays, choughs and nutcrackers make up a family of bold and noisy birds that take their name from the crows, the noisiest of them all. The crows are among the most intelligent of animals, and are capable of solving problems. Were their food supply to disappear for any reason, crows could probably find another supply, whereas less intelligent birds would not know what to do and would starve. Also, scarecrows don't scare crows away after a day or two. Crows often live near to man, finding him a useful source of food, and the birds have inspired many legends. There is a superstition that the Tower of London will stand until its colony of ravens leaves the Tower. Another well-known superstition is that it is unlucky to see only one magpie, but lucky to see a pair.

There are 102 species of crows, and they live throughout the world apart from New Zealand, southern South America and the Antarctic. They are all strong fliers, but only a few northern species migrate.

There are several birds that are individually called crows. The common crow is found in North America, and its counterpart in Europe and Asia is properly called the carrion crow. Similarly, there is the house crow in India and the pied crow in South Africa. They are all large birds, black and grey or black and white in colour, and they all have distinctive cawing voices.

The crows have the largest bodies of all

perching birds, and the largest crow is the raven. It has a length of 26 inches (65 centimetres) and lives throughout the northern hemisphere. The Australian raven is a similar bird, although a different species. The rook is smaller, and the large noisy colonies of nesting rooks are so well-known that the word 'rookery' has come to be used for colonies of other animals, such as seals, as well as for rooks. Rooks live in Europe and Asia. The smaller jackdaw, which is a dark grey bird, also lives in Europe and Asia, and in northern Africa. It is an adaptable bird, and will nest almost anywhere. Other dark-coloured crows include the choughs, which have red or yellow curved beaks and live in Europe and southern and central Asia; and the nutcrackers, which are small and pale grey birds of northern Europe and Asia and North America.

The jays and magpies are much less like each other in appearance than the crows already described. The common jay of Europe and Asia is a pretty bird with a pinkish brown breast and back and a patch of bright blue on its wings. It is 13 inches (33 centimetres) long. It usually lives in woodlands, but is often seen in towns. In America, its counterpart is the blue jay, a bright blue bird with white underparts. The common magpie is found in both the Old World and the New World. It has a black and white body with a long green tail, giving it a total length of 18 inches (46 centimetres). Magpies live in the country, but are sometimes found in towns. They like to steal the eggs of other birds. Several other magpies are brightly coloured; one such bird is the blue magpie of Sri Lanka (Ceylon), which is bright red and blue.

Raven

Clark's nutcracker

Jackdaw

Red-winged Indian cuckoo

Common cuckoo

Cuckoos

The common cuckoo is a famous bird, well-known for its strange two-note call that gives the bird its name in many languages. It is a medium-sized bird, 13 inches (33 centimetres) in length including a long tail. The common cuckoo migrates long distances, arriving in Europe and Asia after wintering in Africa or the East Indies to spend the summer and breed. People look forward to hearing the first cuckoo call as it heralds the arrival of spring. Only the male bird gives the call.

There are 127 different species of cuckoos altogether, although the common cuckoo is the only one that pronounces its name so clearly. It is one of the 42 species of cuckoos in the Old World. All the Old World cuckoos are parasitic in their breeding – that is, they lay their eggs in other birds' nests. A female cuckoo lays several eggs, each one in a different nest. When she is ready to lay, she goes to the nest of one of several species of smaller song-birds

in which the rightful owner has already laid a clutch of eggs. She lifts one of these eggs out with her bill, and lays her own eggs in its place. She then either swallows the egg she has picked up or carries it off and drops it. Cuckoo eggs are bluish or brownish and may be plain or speckled. Each female always lays eggs of the same colour and she usually picks a hostess whose eggs are the same colour as her own.

The young cuckoo hatches either before or at the same time as its foster brothers and sisters, and it quickly sets about removing the other eggs or young birds from the nest. The young cuckoo is going to grow quickly and will need all the food that its foster parents can provide. These foster parents have a natural desire to feed the young, whether they are their own or a young cuckoo. They do this faithfully for about three weeks, after which the young cuckoo is old enough to fend for itself.

The common cuckoo is not a colourful

bird, but some other Old World cuckoos, such as the red-winged Indian cuckoo of India and south-east Asia, are very striking in appearance. The bronze cuckoos of Australia and New Zealand are brownish green with barred black and white underparts.

Unlike their Old World cousins, most New World cuckoos rear their own young. One of the most unusual is the roadrunner, which is 22 inches (56 centimetres) long and lives in the south-western United States and Mexico. It gets its name from the way in which it runs alongside highways, reaching speeds of up to 23 miles (37 kilometres) an hour.

Curlews

See Snipes

Darters

Darters are fresh-water birds of America, Africa, southern Asia and Australasia. They enter the water only to feed and escape from danger. Darters feed in the same way as cormorants, and spread their wings to dry in the same manner because their feathers are not waterproof. They often spend the rest of their time soaring effortlessly above their nesting grounds.

Darters are also known as *anhingas* and as *snake birds*. They get the name of darter from the way in which they dart their beaks at their prey in spear-like thrusts. The name snake bird comes from the way in which they swim, only the head and neck showing above the surface, like a snake swimming through the water. Anhinga is a name that comes from the Indians of the Amazon.

Darters
♂

♀

Dippers

Dippers are the only perching birds that are truly at home in water. They live by cool, rushing streams, diving beneath the water to find water insects, small fish and plants. They can often be seen near waterfalls, behind which they build their nests. As they perch, they constantly bob their heads up and down. There are four species of dippers. The common dipper is a brown bird with a white breast. It lives in Europe, Asia and north-west Africa and is seven inches (18 centimetres) long. Another dipper lives in eastern Asia, and the other two species live in North America and South America.

Common dipper

Divers

Divers are called 'loons' in America, but the first name is more apt because these birds are the champion divers of the bird world. One was once caught in a fisherman's net laid 240 feet (72 metres) below the surface. Divers are known to be able to stay under water for as long as five minutes. But they usually make only shallow dives, staying under water less than a minute – just long enough to catch a fish in their bills.

Divers are built for swimming and diving. They have a streamlined shape. Unlike all other birds, their leg bones are housed inside their bodies down to the ankles. Their webbed feet jut out behind their short tails, rather like twin propellers. The wings are small but, despite this, divers are very good fliers and can reach speeds of up to 60 miles (100 kilometres) an hour. But they have great difficulty in getting airborne. They have to run along the surface for as much as a quarter of a mile (400 metres),

flapping their wings wildly, before getting up enough speed to rise into the air.

However much divers are at home in air and water, they are almost helpless on land. Their feet are just not designed for walking, and they usually squirm about on their breasts.

There are five species of divers, and they breed in the Arctic, coming to the shores or islets of remote lakes to nest. In fact, divers do not actually build nests, but lay their two eggs in a hollow in the ground very near the water. The eggs hatch after a month, and the new-born chicks take to the water with their parents almost at once. When the chicks get tired of swimming, they scramble on to a parent's back for a ride. They learn to dive in about two weeks, but it is a further two months before they can fly. Divers migrate for the winter when the chicks are raised. They fly south to the coasts of Europe, Asia and North America.

Great northern diver

The best known diver is the great northern diver or common loon. It is 36 inches (92 centimetres) long and has a glossy black head and neck with a striped collar and back. The white-billed diver is slightly larger, and, unlike other divers, has a light bill. It stays in northern regions all the year.

Dodos

When Portuguese sailors discovered Mauritius Island in the Indian Ocean in 1507, they found the strange flightless dodo living there. It was about four feet (120 centimetres) long and weighed about 50 pounds (23 kilograms). The dodos ate fruit, seeds and leaves. They nested on the ground, and each female laid a single egg each year. The sailors introduced pigs and monkeys to the island. The sailors killed dodos for food, and the pigs and monkeys feasted on the dodos' eggs. Fewer and fewer dodos were born, and the last dodo died on Mauritius in about 1680. 'As dead as a dodo' is now, alas, a common expression. Two similar birds called solitaires, now also extinct, lived on nearby islands.

Dodo

Domestic Birds

*Domestic pigeons
(different varieties)*

Man makes use of many different kinds of birds. He keeps some kinds in permanent captivity and breeds them for their special qualities. These birds, such as chickens and pigeons, are domestic birds. Birds such as cormorants and falcons that fish and hunt for their masters are not really domestic birds. Although they are tamed, they are captured in the wild rather than bred in captivity.

Pigeons are domestic birds that are raised mainly for food. But the pigeon's homing ability has been known for thousands of years, and today people raise homing pigeons for racing. Racing pigeons can fly at an average speed of about 50 miles (80 kilometres) an hour! Domestic pigeons are all descended from the rock pigeon, which lives in the wild in Europe, Asia and northern

White domestic goose

Peking duck

Africa. The rock pigeon was probably first domesticated in Iraq as early as 4500 BC for use in religious ceremonies. The pharaohs of Egypt, Julius Caesar and Napoleon all used homing pigeons as carriers.

Chickens are raised not only for their meat and eggs, but also for their appearance. Poultry fanciers breed chickens with specially magnificent plumage. Chickens are also bred for the fighting qualities of the cocks. The chicken was domesticated soon after the pigeon and, like the pigeon, was used in religious ceremonies. Domestic chickens are all descended from the jungle fowl of southeast Asia.

Guinea fowl were probably domesticated by the ancient Greeks and Romans. They live in the wild in Africa, but are raised in many countries for their meat. Turkeys live in the wild in Mexico and the south-eastern United States. They were domesticated by the Indians of Mexico long before the Spanish conquerors first brought turkeys to Europe about AD 1500.

Geese were domesticated shortly after chickens. The grey-lag goose of Europe and Asia is the ancestor of most domestic geese, even the white farmyard goose, which is an albino or white form of the grey-lag goose. Ducks were domesticated in China about 400 BC. Today's common domestic ducks are descended from the green-headed mallard of the northern hemisphere. Ducks were probably first bred in China, the Peking duck being named after the Chinese capital. The muscovy duck, another domestic duck, lives in the wild in South and Central America and, like the turkey, was first domesticated by the Indians there.

Several pheasants and partridges are semi-domesticated. Although not in captivity, their breeding is encouraged and controlled by man. Peacocks are raised as ornamental birds, and quails are kept for their eggs and meat.

Ostriches have been kept not only for their plumes, but also to carry people and pull carts. Many cagebirds are bred in captivity for their appearance as well as for their voices.

Muscovy duck ♂

Doves
See Pigeons

Ducks
See Domestic Birds;
Wildfowl

Harpy eagle

Eagles

All through history, nations, rulers and conquerors have chosen eagles as their emblem and displayed them on their flags and banners. These magnificent birds of prey, with their sharply hooked beaks and beady eyes, have an air of grim savagery and beauty. Eagles soar effortlessly through the air in search of their prey far below, diving down in relentless pursuit. They are not the largest birds of prey, being smaller than the ugly and awkward vultures and the rare condors, but they are the most majestic.

The royal house of ancient Babylonia used an eagle as its symbol of state 6000 years ago. This was probably the golden eagle, found around the world north of the equator although it is now a rare bird. The golden eagle is in fact light brown rather than gold in colour, and it measures 33 inches (84 centimetres) in length.

The bald eagle is the national bird of the United States of America, although it

Golden eagle

Bald eagle

is found also in Canada. Slightly larger than the golden eagle, it is not bald but has a head of white feathers. Its favourite food is fish, which it sometimes obtains by forcing an osprey (another bird of prey and a good fisherman) to drop its catch! So swift is the bald eagle in flight that it has the fish in its talons long before it hits the ground or water below.

Eagles are found in most parts of the world. The harpy eagle of Central and South America is even larger than the bald eagle. It lives in the rain forests, swooping through the branches in pursuit of monkeys, sloths and tropical birds. Several kinds of eagles are called sea eagles. The red-backed sea eagle of Australia and Asia is a handsome bird with a white head and breast and golden-brown back and wings. It lives on sea coasts, in mangrove swamps and along beaches and rocky shores.

See also HAWKS.

Egrets

See Herons

Emus

*See Ostriches and Other
Ratite Birds*

Falcons

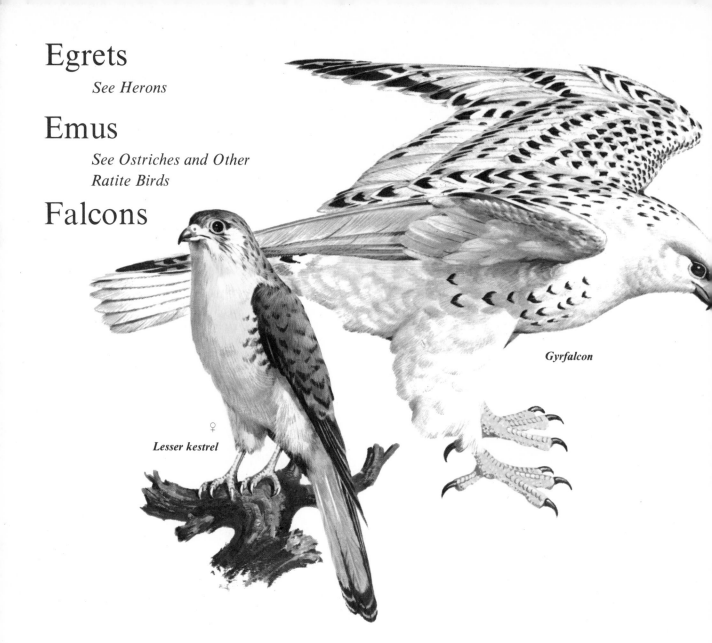

Lesser kestrel

Gyrfalcon

Falcons are birds of prey. They have long pointed wings, large black eyes above sharply-hooked short beaks, and rather long legs with strong hooked talons. In many falcons, the upper bill has a notch that resembles a tooth. There are 58 species of falcons, varying in size from the pygmy falconet, which is six and a half inches (16 centimetres) long to the gyrfalcon, which has a length of 24 inches (60 centimetres). Falcons do not build nests, but lay their eggs on the ground or on cliff ledges. Sometimes they use the old nests of crows and other birds. Most falcons nest by themselves.

But the lesser kestrel of Europe breeds in colonies of up to 100 pairs in holes in old walls or trees.

Falcons seek their prey – small mammals, birds, reptiles and large insects – from a high perch or in flight far above the ground. Then they swoop rapidly towards their victim. The peregrine falcon, which is found throughout the world except in New Zealand, can dive at a speed of 175 miles (280 kilometres) an hour. It makes a clean kill, striking its prey with its talons as it passes. Training falcons to perch on the wrist and to hunt at an order is an unusual hobby.

Feathers

Millions of years ago, birds slowly evolved from reptiles, which are covered with scales. Birds still have scales on their legs, and it is probable that feathers developed from scales. Feathers, scales, horns, antlers, hair, claws and nails are all made of a horny substance called keratin. Like hair and nails, feathers can be trimmed without causing pain. But a trimmed feather does not keep growing like hair and nails do; when a feather reaches its full size it stops growing.

Feathers are far more important to birds than hair and nails are to us. They enable birds to fly, giving them the ability to move up and through the air and to steer in flight. Feathers also protect birds from great heat and cold. The feathers trap a layer of air against the bird's skin, insulating the bird against heat and cold. The appearance of a bird depends on the colour, size and shape of its feathers, and appearance is vital to the life of a bird.

Birds have several different kinds of feathers. The feathers that give a bird its shape are called contour feathers. They have a stiff central shaft from which many barbs sprout. The barbs have smaller barbules, which have hooks and attach themselves to other barbules. In this way, the barbs mesh together to produce the vane on each side of the shaft. Down feathers are very short, soft feathers worn under the contour feathers. Newly hatched chicks are covered with down feathers. A bird keeps its feathers in order by dipping its bill into the preen gland just above its tail, and smoothing or preening its feathers with oil from the gland. Herons have special feathers called powder-down feathers

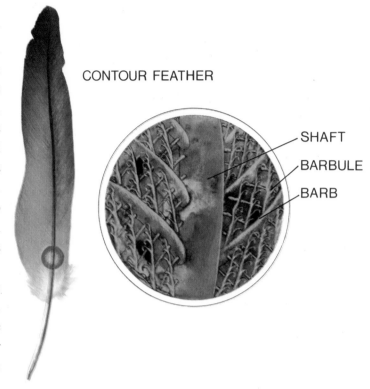

CONTOUR FEATHER

SHAFT
BARBULE
BARB

that produce a fine powder. The birds use this powder to clean their plumage. They apply the powder to their feathers and comb it out with a claw; it picks up slime and dirt.

Birds change their feathers. Many grow new patterns of plumage for the breeding season and then change back afterwards. Also, birds must lose their old, worn feathers and grow new ones. This is called moulting. A few birds change their plumage to match changes in their surroundings. Several Arctic birds wear brown feathers in summer to match the earth and white in winter to match the snow.

How many feathers does a bird possess? This depends on the bird's size and the time of year, for a bird has more feathers in winter than in summer. Even the smallest bird has at least a thousand feathers. One ornithologist plucked a dead swan and counted more than 25,000 feathers!

Finches

Bullfinch
♂

Gouldian finch
♂

Siskin
♂

Woodpecker finch
♂

Finches make up a large group of small perching birds that eat seeds. There are two main groups of finches: the 138 species of goldfinches and related finches and the 108 species of weaver finches or waxbills. The goldfinches include the chaffinch, goldfinch, bullfinch and canary. They live throughout the world except in Australia, although some species have been introduced there. The waxbills are tropical birds of the Old World and many of them are brightly coloured. The sparrow may look like a finch, but it belongs to the weaverbirds. In America, some finches are called sparrows and other birds such as buntings, cardinals and tanagers are called finches!

The European goldfinch is one of the prettiest of the finches. It is not gold all over but is brown, black and white with a red face and a golden stripe along its wings. The European goldfinch is five and a half inches (13 centimetres) long and lives in Asia and north-west Africa as well as in Europe. More like a golden finch is the siskin, a slightly smaller bird of the cooler parts of Europe and Asia. It has a beautiful

Zebra finch
♂

European goldfinch
♂

Yellow-bellied waxbill
♂

Avadavat
♂

yellow breast with yellow patches on its head and wings. The bullfinch is found in the same regions as the siskin, but is larger. It has a fine dusky pink breast and its back and wings are grey and white. An unusual group of finches are the finches found in the Galapagos Islands. The birds that live on different islands have evolved slightly different features and habits. Darwin studied them when he formulated his theory of evolution, and so they are called Darwin's finches. One of them, the woodpecker finch, uses a twig or cactus spine to help catch insects. This is a very unusual example of an animal using a tool. Finches described in other entries in this book include CANARIES, CHAFFINCHES, CROSSBILLS, and GROSBEAKS.

The waxbills or weaver finches are popular cage birds because of their bright colours and lively nature. They include the gouldian finch and the zebra finch of Australia, and the avadavat of India and south-east Asia. The yellow-bellied waxbill lives in southern Africa. Waxbills are from three to six inches (seven to 15 centimetres) in length.

Flamingos

The flamingo is a very beautiful bird with its soft pink plumage and long, elegant neck and legs. Flamingos live in flocks in shallow waters, either at the sea shore or on inland lakes. Flocks of flamingos may contain more than a million birds. They make a spectacular sight, feeding head down in the water or flying in a pink cloud through the sky.

The bill of the flamingo is different from that of every other bird. Instead of having teeth, the bill contains plates with small slits rather like combs. The flamingo sucks water through the plates, and small water plants and animals are caught in them – just like in a strainer. The flamingo then eats these plants and animals. The tongue of the flamingo is too large to enable it to swallow fish.

There are four species of flamingos. The greater flamingo, which is 50 inches (127 centimetres) long, is found in South and Central America, Africa and southern Asia. There are two colonies in Europe – one at the Camargue nature reserve in southern France and the other in southern Spain. These colonies migrate across the Mediterranean Sea to Africa. There they join the great flocks of lesser flamingoes, which live only in the lakes of the rift valleys of Africa. Lesser flamingoes are smaller than greater flamingos, have darker bills and redder plumage. The plumage of greater flamingos varies in colour depending on the food they eat. In the West Indies they are deep pink, but in other places they are often white with pink tails, bills and legs. The other two species of flamingos live in the Andes mountains of South America.

Flamingos make a nest of mud that dries hard in the sun. They lay one white egg, which takes a month to hatch. The new-born flamingo chick has grey down and is hardly as big as its parents' strange bills. But it has a pink bill and legs. The young flamingos are strong enough to leave the nest only three or four days after hatching. They start to feed themselves after three weeks.

Greater flamingos

Flycatchers

Flycatchers are not only good at catching flies, but feed on all kinds of insects. They are small to medium birds, and the flycatchers that live in the New World differ from those that live in the Old World. The New World flycatchers are called tyrant flycatchers by ornithologists. There are 365 species and they nearly all live in trees throughout North, Central and South America. These flycatchers dart after insects in brief rapid flights, snap them up in their bills and return to their perches to eat. New World flycatchers have various names, such as the eastern Phoebe and eastern kingbird. Some have crests, such as the great crested flycatcher. The scissor-tailed flycatcher, with its long, trailing tail, is the largest tyrant flycatcher. With its tail, it has an overall length of 15 inches (37 centimetres).

The flycatchers of the Old World are entirely different to the tyrant flycatchers. They are closely related to babblers, thrushes and warblers. But they live almost entirely on insects.

Like most of the New World flycatchers, the Old World flycatchers are usually plain brown or grey birds. The common spotted flycatcher, for example, is dark brown above and light buff below. It is six inches (15 centimetres) long and lives in Europe, Asia and north-west Africa. But some flycatchers of the Old World are very spectacular in appearance. The paradise flycatchers of Asia and Africa have long trailing tails, crests on their heads, and are coloured brightly.

The birds that Australians call robins are in fact flycatchers. But unlike the robin redbreast, these Australian robins are mostly grey in colour.

Scissor-tailed flycatcher

Great crested flycatcher

Eastern Phoebe

Eastern kingbird

Fowls

Chachalaca

Jungle fowl

♂

We probably think of a fowl as another name for a chicken. But to ornithologists, 240 other birds are called fowls. Like chickens, they are mostly ground birds and good to eat. They include the strange mound builders, such as the mallee fowl. Then there are curassows, such as the chachalaca of tropical America, grouse, partridges, and pheasants, including the jungle fowl – the wild ancestor of domestic chickens, guinea fowls, turkeys and hoatzins.

Frigate Birds

With their huge wings, which can be as much as 90 inches (230 centimetres) across, frigate birds soar effortlessly above the sea. They rarely land on the sea or rest on the ground because of the difficulty they would have getting back into the air. Frigate birds roost in trees or in other high places, so that they can simply drop from their perches to become airborne. They eat by snatching

42

fish and other animals from the surface of the sea. They also steal from gulls and other sea birds by forcing them to drop their catches, and are also known as man-o-war birds for this reason. Frigate birds also prey on colonies of nesting sea birds, diving from the sky to snatch up helpless chicks.

There are five species of frigate birds and they live around the coasts and islands of tropical seas. The magnificent frigate bird is the largest species. All male frigate birds have a breast pouch that turns bright red in the courting season. The male inflates this pouch so that it puffs up like a balloon to attract the female bird.

Magnificent frigate birds

Gannets

Gannets are sea birds the size of geese with sharp beaks and fierce-looking eyes. They feed by diving into the sea and chasing fish underwater. Three species of gannets live in cooler waters – the northern gannet of the North Atlantic, the Cape gannet of South Africa and the Australian gannet of Australia and New Zealand.

The other six species of gannets are called boobies. They got this name because boobies, not being scared of man, can easily be caught. They are natural victims for 'booby traps'. Boobies live in warm tropical seas. As well as diving for fish, they follow ships to catch flying fish fleeing from the ships' bows. These birds live around the world.

Blue-faced booby

Brown booby

Geese

See Wildfowl

Gnatcatchers

Gnatcatchers and goldcrests, which are closely related, belong to the warbler family. They are small birds, about four inches (ten centimetres) long, which live in trees, eating the small insects to be found on the leaves. The firecrest is a goldcrest found in Europe. It has a beautiful orange and yellow patch on the crown of its head. In America, goldcrests are called kinglets. The ruby-crowned kinglet of North America has a red head patch. Gnatcatchers are found only in the New World. A typical gnatcatcher is the blue-grey gnatcatcher of North and Central America.

Firecrest

Ruby-crowned kinglet

Blue-grey gnatcatcher

Grebes

Grebes are elegant water birds with slender necks and long, pointed bills. They breed on lakes and rivers throughout the world and some species migrate to coasts in winter. They are not good fliers, but they are very much at home in water. Grebes dive for their food, and dive rather than fly away from danger. They can hide by submerging their bodies until just their eyes are above the surface.

There are 21 species of grebes. The red-necked grebe lives throughout the northern hemisphere. The great-crested

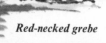

Red-necked grebe

grebe of the Old World can be identified by its black head crest and rusty mane around its neck. Some species of grebes are found only on remote lakes high up in the Andes mountains in South America.

Grebes are famous for their elaborate courtship dances. Great-crested grebes perform a 'penguin dance' in which they rear up facing each other with pieces of weed in their mouths. The pair of grebes build a nest together, constructing a floating heap of water plants. When the chicks are born, the parents carry them about on their backs. They even dive with the young aboard, and if some of the chicks lose their grip, they bob up to the surface of the water without any harm.

Grebes are unusual because they eat some of their own feathers and feed them to their chicks. It may be that the feathers help the grebe's digestion.

Grosbeaks

Two kinds of birds are called grosbeaks because of their heavy, strong beaks. Some are related to goldfinches and the others to cardinals and buntings, but they are very similar in general appearance. The evening grosbeak is an American bird of the first group. It comes to feeding trays for sunflower seeds in the winter. The pine grosbeak is also related to the goldfinches, and lives in northern evergreen forests around the world. It is large for a finch, being nine inches (23 centimetres) long. The grosbeaks of the second group live only in the New World. The rose-breasted grosbeak and the blue grosbeak are fine singing birds often seen in gardens in America.

Blue grosbeak
♂

Evening grosbeak
♂

Rose-breasted grosbeak
♂

Grouse

Grouse are medium to large birds which live only in the northern hemisphere. There are 18 species, including four species of ptarmigans. Grouse and ptarmigans have feathers over their ankles, and some ptarmigans have their toes covered with feathers as well. Ptarmigans live in cold climates, and the feathers keep their feet warm and help them to walk on soft snow. Most grouse and ptarmigans also have a patch of brightly-coloured bare skin above each eye.

In the spring, many male grouse perform elaborate courting dances. The

Rock ptarmigan (summer plumage)

(winter plumage)

Prairie chicken

prairie chicken of North America gathers with other males at special courtship grounds on the prairies. The males run about rapidly and pivot in circles, spreading their fan-like tails. They utter loud booming calls, puff up orange air sacs on their necks and raise crests of feathers on their heads. The capercaillie and the black grouse of Europe and Asia are dark-coloured birds which behave in a similar way.

Other male grouse prefer to attract their females alone. The ruffed grouse of North America stands on a log and

beats its wings rapidly to and fro. This produces a noise like a thunderous drum roll. The male or cock takes only one mate, unlike most other cock grouse, which have a harem of from two to 15 females or hens. The hens raise the chicks without the help of the cocks and the chicks may stay with their mothers throughout the summer.

Ptarmigans are slightly smaller than grouse. The rock ptarmigan and the willow grouse, which is in fact a ptarmigan, live in northern lands around the North Pole. But the rock ptarmigan is also found as far south as the Pyrenees mountains, the Alps and Japan. The

Ruffed grouse

white-tailed ptarmigan lives in the northern regions of North America. These three ptarmigans change their plumage with the seasons. In winter they are white; in summer they become mostly brown. These seasonal changes protect the birds from enemies, because they are almost invisible against the white snow in winter and against the brown earth in summer. The fourth ptarmigan is the red grouse, which lives on moors in Britain and Ireland. It stays the same reddish brown colour throughout the year, but as there is little snow where it lives, the red grouse does not need to change colour.

Grouse and ptarmigans are a favourite target for hunters. The hunters often use dogs to make the birds fly into the air, where they can easily be shot. But shooting is allowed only at certain times of year, so that grouse are left to breed undisturbed.

Guillemots
See Auks

Vulturine guinea fowl

Helmeted guinea fowl

Guinea Fowl

Africa, south of the Sahara Desert, and the island of Madagascar are the homes of the ten species of guinea fowl. Guinea fowl are raised as domestic birds for their tasty flesh in many countries. These domestic guinea fowl are all descended from the wild helmeted guinea fowl of West Africa. The domestic bird is very similar to the wild bird in appearance.

The largest guinea fowl is the vulturine guinea fowl. It is 30 inches (75 centimetres) long and lives in East Africa. It gets its name because its head resembles that of a vulture.

Guinea fowl feed and nest on the ground but roost in trees at night. They like each other's company and travel around in flocks of a hundred or more birds. Guinea fowl usually run from danger.

Arctic tern

Black tern

Sooty tern

Gulls

Gulls are a common sight at the sea shore. They wheel about in small flocks, scavenging for food with shrill cries and screams. Gulls are not great fishermen, preferring to get their food by following ships and snatching up garbage dumped overboard. They clean harbours and beaches of refuse, and will also come inland to eat at rubbish dumps and look for insects and worms.

There are 43 species of gulls and they live at sea coasts in cooler waters around the world. They are grouped in the same family of birds as the 39 species of terns. Gulls and terns are all various shades of white, black, grey and brown. But it is easy to tell the difference between gulls and terns by looking at their bills. A gull has a stout bill with a strong hook, whereas the bill of a tern is narrow and pointed.

Terns usually live in warmer waters than gulls. Both gulls and terns nest in colonies on cliffs and offshore islands, and some species nest on inland lakes and marshes. Many gulls have a bright red patch on their bills. This patch is important in feeding the young. The chick pecks at the patch and this action makes the parent feed the chick.

The largest gulls are the great black-backed gull of the North Atlantic and Mediterranean Sea, and the Pacific gull of South Australia. Their wingspans may stretch to five feet (150 centimetres). Both birds are similar in appearance, being white with black upper wings. Herring gulls, one of the best known gulls, will eat almost anything. They have been known to pick up golf balls and try to eat them! Like some other gulls, herring gulls may eat shellfish by picking up one in its bill and dropping it from the air on to a rock to break open the shell.

Like the herring gull, the kittiwake is found throughout the northern hemisphere. But unlike other gulls, the kittiwake often flies out of sight of land. It follows fishing fleets across the ocean, whereas other gulls usually turn back after a few miles. The kittiwake is the only gull that swims underwater in pursuit of small fish.

Some unusual gulls include the ivory gull of the Arctic, which is pure white, and the lava gull of the Galapagos Islands, which is completely grey.

Terns differ from gulls not only in their bills but also in their behaviour. Whereas gulls are scavengers, terns are more choosy about their food. They dive from the air to catch small fish, squid, and shrimps below the surface of the water. Inland terns often catch insects on the wing. Terns are also the champion long-distance fliers of the bird world. Gulls do not usually travel very far.

The Arctic tern breeds in or near the Arctic during the summer months. Then, in August or September, it migrates south along the coasts of America or Africa or over the Atlantic Ocean. Some Arctic terns travel as far as the Antarctic and spend what are then the summer months there before returning north to breed. These birds migrate about 22,000 miles (35,000 kilometres) every year in these two great journeys, a record distance. Because the sun never sets during the summer months near the Poles, the Arctic tern may spend as long as ten months a year in perpetual daylight. The black tern breeds on inland marshes in Europe, Asia and North America. The sooty tern nests on tropical islands but spends the rest of its life entirely at sea on the wing. As the sooty tern cannot swim and never alights on the water, it must be able to rest or sleep as it soars.

Kittiwake

Great black-backed gull

Herring gull

Bataleur eagle

Swallow-tailed kite

Hawks

Hawks, eagles, kites, harriers and Old World vultures all make up a single family of 205 species of birds of prey. They live in all parts of the world except Antarctica, and range in size from small hawks the size of a pigeon to the lammergeyer or bearded vulture. This huge bird of Africa, southern Europe and central Asia is four feet (120 centimetres) long and has a wingspan of up to ten feet (300 centimetres). The lammergeyer has an unusual way of eating. It eats carrion, but waits until other vultures have finished with a carcass before eating. It then eats the bones, dropping some from the air to break them open.

With the exception of the vultures, the hawks and their relatives mostly eat live animals. They sit high on a perch or soar in the sky, their beady eyes trained on the ground beneath. Their vision is so perfect that they can easily spot their prey far below, when they swoop down in pursuit. The birds kill with a slash of their sharp claws as they pass or capture the animal in their talons and then tear it apart with their short hooked bills. These hawks eat all kinds of small animals, such as rats, mice, squirrels, rabbits, lizards, snakes, frogs, snails, and insects.

Except for the harriers, male and female hawks look alike, but the females are larger than the males. All hawks have feathers on the upper parts of their rather long legs. When they perch or walk, they look as if they are wearing short, feathered trousers.

Apart from the ground-nesting harriers and some kites, hawks nest high in trees, on rock ledges or on cliffs. They build bulky nests of sticks and bark, often using them year after year. Males and females mate for life and raise from one to six chicks a year.

Kites are graceful hawks that sail through the air with ease. The swallow-tailed kite has a forked tail like a swallow.

Hen harrier

Red-tailed hawk

Cooper's hawk

Goshawk

It also swoops about rather like a swallow. It once lived throughout the New World, but is now a rare bird as many have been killed by hunters. The honey buzzard of the Old World is a close relative of the swallow-tailed kite. Other Old World kites include the brahminy kite of India, south-east Asia and Australia. It is a handsome reddish brown bird with a white head. Like the black kite of Europe and Asia, it sometimes scavenges for food at rubbish dumps and harbours.

Most of the birds called hawks are very good hunters. The goshawk of the northern hemisphere was used in medieval Japan to hunt cranes, although the latter are much larger birds. Cooper's hawk of North America and the sparrowhawk of Europe are small hawks less than a foot (about 30 centimetres) long, but they do sometimes steal poultry from farm-yards. The larger hawks are often called buzzards. They include the red-

tailed hawk of America, which is very similar to the common buzzard of Europe and Asia. These birds catch rats and so are beneficial to man.

The harriers are another group of hawks. They are called harriers because they harry their prey, flying low back and forth over fields or marshes in search of food. The hen harrier lives in the northern hemisphere, and is called the marsh hawk in America. The male is grey and the female brown.

As a group, the eagles are the largest hawks. Related to them is another group of smaller eagles called serpent eagles. They get this name because snakes are their favourite food, but they eat other reptiles and amphibians, which they find on marshy ground. The bataleur eagle is a serpent eagle of Africa. It is an aerial acrobat, and often performs somersaults in mid-air.

See also BUZZARDS, EAGLES, FALCONS, OSPREYS, VULTURES.

Herons

Black-crowned night heron

Quiet shallow waters in rivers, marshes, lakes and seas are the homes of the 64 different birds of the heron family. In all but the icy lands near the poles and some islands, they wade and catch fish, crabs, insects, amphibians, reptiles, rats and mice. Using their straight long bills, they pierce their prey and then swallow it whole.

The heron family contains egrets, night herons and bitterns as well as herons. These birds have long S-shaped necks and long legs in addition to their long bills, giving herons and egrets an elegant, stately appearance. The night herons and bitterns are more stocky birds, and the shape of the neck is often hidden among its plumage. Under their outer feathers, all herons have patches of an unusual down that flakes off into powder. The birds dip their bills or heads into these patches of powder down and apply it to their feathers. The powder soaks up slime and grease, and then the birds comb out the dirty powder with their claws. People use a dry shampoo in exactly the same way!

Bitterns nest on or very near the ground, whereas other herons nest in trees. Birds that breed in temperate regions migrate to warmer parts for the winter, but the herons of the tropics do not migrate.

The birds named herons are the tallest and most beautiful members of the heron family. The great blue heron of North America and the very similar common heron or grey heron of Europe, Asia and Africa stand as high as five feet (150 centimetres). They nest in colonies in tall trees, and these heronries may contain 100 nests. Another beautiful heron is the slightly smaller purple

Cattle egret

Little blue heron
♂

Great blue heron
♂

Reddish egret
♂

American bittern

heron of Europe, Africa and Asia, which gets its name from its purple wings.

Egrets are usually smaller than herons and have delicate, airy plumes during the breeding season. These birds are also sometimes called herons. For example, the world-wide common egret is also called the great white heron; and the reddish egret and the little blue heron of the New World are closely related birds. In fact, the little blue heron is white for the first year of its life and looks very like the snowy egret of the New World. The little

egret of the Old World is very similar to the snowy egret. Egrets were killed for their plumes in the 18th and 19th centuries, but the slaughter of these birds is now against the law. The world-wide cattle egret gets its name from the way in which it follows cattle, eating the insects they disturb.

Night herons get their name because they sleep during the day and fish at night. The black-crowned night heron is found in most parts of the world. In Japan, this bird is called the 'goi sagi',

Snowy egret

meaning 'heron of the fifth imperial rank'. The Emperor Daigo knighted it in the year AD 930 because of its beauty and tameness.

Bitterns live in reedy marshes, and their plumage exactly matches their surroundings. Bitterns escape danger by freezing and remaining stock-still, whereas most other herons escape by flight. Young black-crowned night herons look like bitterns, but are usually smaller. It is possible to be within touching distance of a bittern, yet still not be able to spot it.

Male bitterns make strange booming calls at night during the spring to attract the females. The sound carries a long way over the marshes. There are two groups of bitterns, large and small. The large bitterns are about the size of a cockerel. They are all very similar and include the American bittern and the common bittern of the Old World. Small bitterns are about a foot (30 centimetres) long and are the smallest members of the heron family. In America, these birds are called least bitterns and elsewhere little bitterns.

Hoatzins

Hoatzin and young

The hoatzin is a fascinating bird. When a hoatzin chick hatches, it has two claws on each wing. The chick crawls about and uses its claws to climb trees. The first prehistoric bird, archaeopteryx, had similar wing claws and some scientists have debated whether the hoatzin is a missing link between prehistoric and modern birds. But other scientists believe that its claws may have developed since prehistoric times. The claws disappear when the feathers grow.

Hoatzins live on the banks of rivers in the Amazon Basin of South America, building frail nests over the water. Hoatzins mainly eat the rubbery leaves of a tall arum tree that the people there call 'mucca-mucca'. Hoatzins have enormous crops in which the leaves are partly digested. The chick takes food from the crop. Hoatzins cannot really fly; they clamber to the top of a mucca-mucca tree, eating as they climb. At the top they flop into the air and half fall and half glide to the bottom of another.

Honeycreepers

There are 22 species of the small Hawaiian honeycreepers, and they are found only in Hawaii. Different species have evolved to suit the differing conditions on the various islands. Some honeycreepers, as their name suggests, feed mainly on nectar and have long, curving bills to probe plants. Others tear away bark on trees to get at insects, and their bills are hooked. Some are seed eaters and have strong, parrot-like bills. Male honeycreepers are brightly coloured in reds, yellows and greens, whereas the females are duller. Birds that evolve special features to suit certain habitats tend to die out when their surroundings change. Several species of Hawaiian honeycreepers have therefore become extinct and some are still in danger.

Hawaiian honeycreeper

Red-legged honeycreeper

Honeyeaters

Tui

Helmeted honeyeater

Honeyeaters are thought of as the most Australian of all birds. There are 165 species living in Australia, New Zealand and the surrounding islands. Honeyeaters have long tongues that can be rolled into tubes for sucking up nectar from plants. As well as nectar they eat insects and fruit. Honeyeaters vary in size from four to 15 inches (ten to 38 centimetres). They are mostly dull-coloured with yellowish heads, like the helmeted honeyeater of south-eastern Australia. But the cardinal honeyeater and scarlet honeyeaters are brilliant red birds. On Santa Cruz, a Pacific island, belts made of red honeyeater feathers are used as money. The tui of New Zealand is a handsome green honeyeater that can sing well and mimic the sounds may be animals. It is 11 inches (23 centimetres) long.

Honeyguides

Honeyguides, particularly the greater honeyguide of Africa, get their name from the amazing way in which they guide animals and sometimes men to bees' nests. Honeyguides can digest bees' wax, but they cannot open the nests by themselves. They therefore guide a honey badger or other animal – even a man – to the nest by leading them there with chattering calls. The badger or the man opens the nest and gets the honey and the honeyguide gets the wax!

There are 12 species of honeyguides, which are small, dull-coloured birds of Africa and Asia. They lay their eggs in the nests of other birds. The newly-hatched honeyguide has sharp hooks on the tips of its bill, which it uses to kill the other chicks in the nest.

Greater honeyguide

Hoopoes

An old legend says that the hoopoe was given its crown by King Solomon. It was a reward for shading the monarch from the desert sun with its outspread wings. Hoopoes seem to delight in their crests, raising and lowering them as they fly erratically through the air and walk about the ground, pecking for worms and insects.

Hoopoes nest in holes in trees, banks and in old buildings. The female stays with the newly-hatched chicks all the time while the male hunts food for the family. Hoopoes are bad housekeepers and never clean out their nest-holes.

Hoopoes live in Europe, Asia and Africa and make up a single species. The 16 species of wood hoopoes of Africa, which are a separate family, have no crests.

Hoopoe

Hornbills

Hornbills are famous for their great down-curving bills, which are often the same buff colour as the horns of cattle. But the bills may also be black, yellow or red, and there may be a great protruding casque on top of the bill, as in the black-casqued hornbill of Africa. There are 45 species of hornbills. They have black and white plumage and live in the forests and grasslands of tropical Asia and Africa. They are large birds, ranging in size from one and a half to five and a half feet (45 to 170 centimetres). The great hornbill of south-eastern Asia often has a yellowish appearance because of the bright yellow oil from its preening gland with which it covers itself.

Hornbills are usually seen early in the morning or in the evening when it is cool. They hunt for berries, fruit, grain, insects, young birds, eggs and snakes. Some hornbills follow columns of ants, hopping about on the ground trying to catch them. Hornbills fly strongly, their wings thrashing the air with strokes that sound like the puffs of an old steam engine. They call with honks, squeals, whistles and laughs.

When hornbills are ready to nest, the female enters a nesting hole in a tree and seals herself in, using mud and droppings as plaster. She remains there for a month to 40 days until the eggs hatch, and then a further two to four weeks until the chicks are half-grown. A small hole is left in the wall so that the female can poke out her bill for food, which the male faithfully brings. This strange habit protects the eggs and young from monkeys and snakes. It also protects the female bird, as she moults her feathers inside her nesting hole and is helpless until the new feathers grow.

Great hornbill

Black-casqued hornbill

Hummingbirds

If emeralds, rubies, sapphires, amethysts and all the other precious stones grew wings and flew, they might rival the gleaming male hummingbirds. Their glistening, iridescent plumage has given many hummingbirds the names of gems, such as the ruby topaz, the amethyst-throated, the blue-chinned sapphire and the glittering-bellied emerald hummingbirds. The females are less striking. The female ruby-throated hummingbird resembles her mate, but she does not have his beautiful ruby throat.

In the 19th century, millions of hummingbird skins were shipped to Europe from South America and the West Indies to be worn as ornaments. But, fortunately, hummingbird skins do not last as well as precious stones. If this were not so, many of the 319 species of hummingbirds would now be extinct.

Hummingbirds are all small birds. The Cuban bee hummingbird of the West Indies is the smallest bird in the world. It is only two and a quarter inches (six centimetres) long from the tip of its bill to the tip of its tail. And it weighs only as much as a quarter of a teaspoonful of sugar! No hummingbird has a body longer than four inches (ten centimetres). The giant hummingbird is twice as long, but half its length is taken up by its bill and tail. The swordbilled and the stream-ertail hummingbirds are even longer,

Swordbilled hummingbird ♂

Ruby-throated hummingbirds ♂ ♀

Giant hummingbird ♂

Streamertail hummingbird ♂

Blue-throated hummingbird ♂

Ruby topaz hummingbird ♂

Rufous hummingbird ♂

but one has a magnificent spear of a bill and the other two lovely trailing plumes for a tail.

Hummingbirds live only in the New World, and most of them live in the tropical regions. But the rufous hummingbird breeds as far north as southern Alaska and the Chilean fire-crown breeds as far south as Tierra del Fuego.

Hummingbirds get their name because they can move their wings to and fro so fast that a low hum is produced. The wings move so quickly that the human eye sees only a blur. The hummingbird cannot glide, but it can fly backwards and hover motionless in the air. Hummingbirds can also keep up this flight for long periods. The ruby-throated hummingbird flies at least 500 miles (800 kilometres) non-stop across the Gulf of Mexico on its way south to spend the winter in Brazil. Its speed has been measured at 30 miles (48 kilometres) an hour, so the journey must take about a day.

Hummingbirds can fly so amazingly because they have large and powerful wing muscles. They eat many insects and the sweet juices of flowers to get energy. A hummingbird can hover in the air before a blossom and insert its slender pointed bill into the flower. The tongue darts from the bill to collect the juice and insects.

When the males of a bird family are more colourful than the females, they are apt to leave the females to raise the young alone. This is the case among the hummingbirds. The female hummingbird weaves a dainty open cup-shaped nest of plant down and spider webs. Two eggs are laid, each as tiny as a quarter of an inch (half a centimetre) long. The young hatch after 14 to 19 days, but then remain in the nest for about three weeks. They must stay this length of time so that they are ready to fly immediately they leave the nest.

Ibises

Ibises are elegant, long-legged wading birds with long, down-curving bills. They live mostly on sand banks, lake shores and marshes where they use their long bills to probe the mud for amphibians, insects and other water creatures. Ibises like each others' company, and travel and breed in flocks. They fly together too, with their necks stretched out in front and their legs trailing behind. Ibises are usually rather quiet birds, but when they raise their voices, they croak harshly or grunt like pigs.

There are 22 kinds of ibises and they vary in length from 20 to 30 inches (50 to 75 centimetres). The ibis that is found in most countries is the glossy ibis. It lives in Europe, Asia, Australia, the southern United States and Central America. It is a fine-looking bird, with shining bronze and purple plumage. The white ibis lives only in the New World. It is slightly larger than the small glossy ibis, and is white all over apart from its red face and legs and brown bill.

Perhaps the best-known ibis, although it is not widespread, is the beautiful scarlet ibis. Its plumage is a vivid red all over, and these birds have been killed in great numbers for their feathers. They are also slaughtered for their meat, although it has an oily, fishy taste. The scarlet ibis was once found in great flocks in the mangrove swamps of tropical South America, but it is now common only in Trinidad.

Another ibis, well-known for its unusual name, is the sacred ibis. It is a white bird, with black head, tail and legs. The sacred ibis is so called because it was worshipped by the ancient Egyptians. Human figures with ibis heads can be seen in Egyptian friezes, representing gods. The birds were mummified and preserved in the tombs of the pharaohs. But these are the only sacred ibises in Egypt today, as this bird now lives south of the Sahara Desert in Africa.

Ibises are grouped in the same bird family as the spoonbills.

White ibis

Glossy ibis

Scarlet ibis

Sacred ibis

American jacana

African jacana

Jacanas

On the marshy edges of lakes and rivers in the tropic lands of the world, the seven species of jacanas walk nimbly on the floating leaves of water lilies and lotus plants. They are also called lily trotters and lotus birds. The name jacana is Portuguese; the *j* is pronounced like the *c* in *cigar*. Jacanas have long toes and claws that spread the birds' weight and prevent them sinking. They also have a thorn-like spur on the bend of each wing. The spurs can serve as weapons with which the jacana defends itself.

Jacanas swim well, diving to escape danger rather than flying away. They usually fly slowly and heavily, with their long feet dangling beneath them, but they can stretch their feet out behind and fly strongly. In the spring the females grow courting plumes and court the males. The nests, made of water plants, float in quiet bays. The males incubate the eggs and raise the chicks, which follow their father to hunt for snails, insects and small fish.

The American jacana is ten inches (25 centimetres) long and wears a reddish yellow head shield above its bill. The African jacana is slightly larger and has a blue head shield.

Jays

See Crows

Kookaburra

Common kingfisher

Belted kingfisher ♂

Malachite kingfisher ♂

White-collared kingfisher

Kingfishers

The most splendid sight a bird watcher can have in Europe is the common kingfisher. Walking along river banks, people watch keenly for this beautiful little bird, with its blue-green wings and orange-red breast. They have to be on the alert, for the kingfisher suddenly darts from a hidden perch down to the water, snatches a fish in its beak, and disappears back to its perch all in less than a second. But, in spite of its name, the common kingfisher is not a common sight. It is one of 80 species of kingfishers which are found in all but the icy regions of the world. The common kingfisher, which is six and a half inches (16 centimetres) long, is found in Asia, Africa and New Guinea as well as in Europe. In North and Central America, its place is taken by the belted kingfisher. This bird is twice the size of the common kingfisher and is greyish blue and white with a brown belt across its chest. Another beautiful kingfisher is the malachite kingfisher of Africa. It has a crest of blue feathers that it raises in alarm or as a display.

When swallowing a fish, kingfishers may turn their catch around with their bills. The bird does this so that it goes down their throats head first and the fins do not scratch its throat. The kingfisher may also beat the fish against its perch to flatten out the fins.

Not all kingfishers hunt fish. A large group of kingfishers live in forests and grasslands, feeding on insects, amphibians, reptiles and perhaps small birds and mammals. The best-known of these forest kingfishers is the kookaburra of Australia. It is among the largest kingfishers, being 17 inches (43 centimetres) long. This bird is also called the laughing kookaburra or laughing jackass, because a group of birds produces a babble of laughs and chuckles as they call. Kookaburras eat snakes and lizards, which they kill by seizing the prey in their mouths and striking it against a branch or by dropping it to the ground. Forest kingfishers may be as beautiful as their fishing relatives. The white-collared kingfisher was a favourite of Chinese jewellers, who used its brilliant blue feathers when making their gems. This forest kingfisher lives in southern Asia, Africa, Australia and many Pacific islands. There are nearly 50 varieties of this bird that differ slightly from region to region.

Fishing kingfishers dig a tunnel into a river bank and nest in the cavity at the end. Forest kingfishers nest in a hole in a tree, a termite mound, or a burrow which they dig into a bank or a cliff.

Kites

See Hawks

Kiwis

*See Ostriches and
Other Ratite Birds*

Skylark

Horned lark

Larks

The skylark is the best-known of this family of 70 birds. It is famous for its musical song, which it performs as it flutters through the air. Skylarks live naturally in Europe, Asia and North Africa. But people have become so enraptured by it that they have taken it to other parts of the world. Skylarks have been introduced into New Zealand, Hawaii and Canada.

Like other larks, skylarks are drab birds. They are streaked with brown and grey on top and are lighter beneath. But larks usually live on the ground and not in trees, and their dull plumage camouflages them perfectly among the grass of the moors, plains and fields where they live. Larks walk or run about the ground instead of hopping like most other birds. They build mostly open, cup-shaped nests. The female bird incubates the two to six white speckled eggs for nearly two weeks. The chicks stay in the nest for the same time.

Although larks are found throughout the world, most larks live in Africa. Only one species is found in the New World; this is the horned lark, which has two black tufts of feathers on its head that look like small horns. The horned lark is seven inches (18 centimetres) long, the same size as the skylark.

Lyrebirds

There are two species of lyrebirds, and they both live in the forests of eastern Australia. The family gets its name from the shape of the tail of the male superb lyrebird. Normally the long tail plumes lie behind the bird, but when the male courts the female he raises his tail feathers. The two outer plumes form the shape of the frame of a lyre, an ancient Greek musical instrument like a small harp. The lacy inner plumes form the strings of the lyre. There are two other long plumes that wave gently in the air. The bird holds this pose for a second, and then lowers the plumes over his back. It is a magnificent display, bettering even that of the peacock. The other species of lyrebird is called Albert's lyrebird, and is named after Prince Albert of England. Its tail is not lyre-shaped, but it is closely related to the superb lyrebird.

The female lyrebird does not have a beautiful plumed tail, but she shares another unusual feature with the male. Both birds are excellent mimics. They can accurately imitate the voices of other animals – barking dogs and bleating sheep as well as other birds. They can even reproduce mechanical sounds, like motor horns!

The male plays little part in bringing up the young. The female builds a large dome-shaped nest with a side entrance, and lines the inside with feathers. The single egg takes six weeks to hatch and the chick says inside the nest for another six weeks.

Lyrebirds are the size of cockerels and are the longest perching birds in the world. The males have a total length of 38 inches (97 centimetres), two-thirds of which is taken up by the tail.

Superb lyrebird

♂

Mallee Fowls

The mallee fowl is one of the 12 species of megapodes, or mound builders, which live in Australia and Malaysia. Megapodes are strange birds, because they do not rely on their body warmth to hatch their eggs. Instead of incubating the eggs themselves, the megapodes bury their eggs in heaps of rotting plants, which give off heat, or in hot sand. The chicks hatch inside the mound, and force their way to the surface.

The mallee fowl lives in southern Australia and is two feet (60 centimetres) long. It is a member of the fowl family and resembles a grouse or partridge. The male digs a pit about three feet (about a metre) deep and ten feet (3 metres) across. It fills the pit with wet leaves and grass and covers this with sand to form a mound. Then, about once a week for six months, the male makes a hole and the female lays an egg in the rotting plants. The male covers the hole over and tends the mound continually. He judges the temperature with his tongue, putting on more sand or taking some away to keep the temperature inside exactly the same all the time. After two months, the young chicks start to hatch, one every week. They scramble to the surface of the mound, and are already so well developed that they can look after themselves. Within a day, they can fly!

Yellow-thighed manakin

♂

Bronze-winged manakin

♂

Manakins

Manakins are 59 tiny birds of tropical America, most of them being less than five inches (13 centimetres) long. They live singly or in flocks, and groups of bronze-winged manakins can be seen sitting flank to flank on a branch, preening each other. The call of a manakin does not really sound like that of a bird. It is usually a cracking or rasping noise.

Male manakins have bright patches of colour. The male yellow-thighed manakin has a bright red head and yellow thighs which contrast vividly with its black body. Female manakins are all a drab olive green. The male manakins court the females with eye-catching dances. After mating, the female manakins raise the pair of young alone.

Mynahs

See Starlings

Nenes

See Wildfowl

Nightingales

See Thrushes

Mallee fowl

Nightjars

Nightjars are well named, for their loud, persistent calls can jar the ears at night. The common nightjar of Europe and Asia sounds more like a cricket than a bird, and it sometimes calls for five minutes at a time without pausing between its loud chirps. People have claimed to have heard a nightjar calling more than a thousand times in succession.

There are 70 species of nightjars, and they live around the world except in New Zealand. American nightjars often have strange names, such as chuck-will's-widow and whip-poor-will, which come from the sound of their calls. Nightjars are patterned with browns, blacks, greys and whites. This plumage makes them almost invisible as they sit lengthwise along a branch of a tree or rest among some dead leaves on the ground.

Nightjars have wide mouths with which they catch insects in flight. It was once thought that nightjars sucked milk from goats with their large mouths, and this gave them the name of goatsuckers.

Nightjars usually lay their one or two eggs on the bare ground. The nighthawk, which is not a hawk but an American nightjar, often lays its eggs on a flat roof.

A nightjar called the poor-will of North America and Mexico is the only bird that hibernates through the winter instead of migrating. It crawls into a crack in some rocks and goes to sleep. Its body temperature falls, its heartbeat slows down, and its digestive system stops working until spring comes.

Nighthawk

Whip-poor-will

Nuthatches

In the forests of the northern hemisphere and in Africa and Australia, nuthatches can be seen clinging, head downwards, to the trunks of trees. Their bills probe the bark for insects and spiders, but some nuthatches also eat nuts and seeds. Their names comes from 'nut hacker', as they wedge nuts in crevices in the bark and hack them open. Nuthatches are small birds, three and a half to seven inches (nine to 18 centimetres) long. The common nuthatch of Europe and Asia is buff underneath and grey above. The velvet-fronted nuthatch of south-eastern Asia is a pretty bird with a blue back and white breast.

Most nuthatches nest in holes in trees, which they line with bits of bark, grass and twigs. Sometimes they nest in bird boxes. Some nuthatches, called rock nuthatches, live in rocky mountainous regions in Europe and Asia. They can be seen clinging to rock faces with their heads down, and they make their nests in crevices in the rock.

In Australia, nuthatches are called

Velvet-fronted nuthatch

sittellas from their Latin name *sittidae*. They behave like other nuthatches but they have different nesting habits. Sittellas weave nests of spider webs, cocoons and bark that are difficult to spot among the branches on which they are built.

Orioles

Orioles are small to medium-sized song birds, mostly yellow or orange and black in colour. They build intricate hanging nests. Orioles in the New World are related to tanagers and are different from Old World orioles, which are related to crows. But they do look much the same. In the United States, the Baltimore oriole lives in the eastern states. In the western states, its place is taken by Bullock's oriole. Old World orioles live in Europe, Asia, Africa and Australia.

Bullock's oriole

♂

Baltimore oriole

♂

Ospreys

The osprey is a large fish-eating bird of prey, two feet (60 centimetres) long. It is related to eagles, hawks and falcons, but exists in a family of its own. Ospreys live near lakes, rivers and oceans throughout the world, except in New Zealand. Ospreys that breed in Europe and Asia winter in Africa, the birds in North and Central America migrating to South America. The ospreys that breed in Australia stay there all the year round.

Ospreys circle high in the air over the water and plunge down feet first with wings half-closed when they spot a fish. As they splash into the water, they grab the fish with both feet and carry it, head first, off to a nest or perch. Ospreys are often pestered at their fishing grounds by bald eagles and frigate birds, who force them to drop their catch. In turn, an osprey will drive all hawks and falcons away from its nesting area. In this way, ospreys protect smaller birds around them – including even farmers' poultry.

Osprey

Ospreys have dainty eating habits for a bird of prey. They take small bites of their fish, tearing pieces off with their beaks. After eating, they return to the water and splash around to clean their feet, feathers and beaks.

Ospreys build large, bulky nests of sticks on cliffs and at the tops of trees and telephone poles! The nest is repaired and used year after year, for as long as 40 years. Each year the female lays three white speckled eggs which she incubates for five weeks with some help from her mate. The chicks remain in the nest for two months, the mother feeding them with fish that the father brings.

Although ospreys are harmless, they were driven out of Britain by gamekeepers nearly a century ago. A few pairs of birds tried to return but egg collectors stole their eggs.

Now the nests of any ospreys that come to Britain to breed are fiercely protected by bird lovers.

Ostriches and Other Ratite Birds

The breastbones of most birds are shaped like the keel of a boat. They stick out like the breastbone of a turkey when it is carved at Christmas. The bird's flying muscles are attached to this keel-shaped bone. Some birds which stopped using their wings over a period of millions of years lost their flying muscles. Gradually, the breastbones of these birds flattened out, and they now resemble rafts more than keels. The Latin word for raft is *ratis*, and so these birds are called ratite birds. They are the ostriches, emus, cassowaries and rheas, and the kiwis. More than 40 other kinds of birds no longer fly. But they use their wings for swimming or balancing, and so have not lost the keel on their breastbones.

The ostriches, emus, cassowaries and rheas are similar in appearance and habits although they live a long way apart. The ostrich, a family of one species, is found in southern and eastern Africa and in the Sahara Desert. The emu, another family of one species, lives in Australia. There are three species of cassowaries: the Australian cassowary of Australia and New Guinea, and Bennett's cassowary and the one-wattled cassowary, which are both found only in New Guinea. The two rheas live in South America: the common rhea in Brazil, Uruguay and Argentina, and Darwin's rhea from southern Peru to the straits of Magellan.

These four families of ratite birds are the largest birds in the world. The ostrich is the tallest and heaviest, being eight feet two and a half metres) high. It weighs up to 345 pounds (156 kilograms). The emu is the next largest, and then come the cassowaries. The rheas are the smallest of these birds, but they are still the largest birds of the New World.

All four families have very similar habits. They all eat juicy plants, berries, seeds, fruit and any insects they can find. Their plumage is coloured so that they

Common rhea

Ostrich

Australian cassowary

Emu

Brown kiwi

blend in with their surroundings and escape the attention of enemies. If enemies do come close, their great height enables the birds to spot them easily and they usually escape by running swiftly away. Some ostriches can run at 40 miles (64 kilometres) an hour. The birds can also escape by swimming, even the ostrich whose desert home has little water. The story that ostriches stick their heads in the sand to hide from danger is nonsense. It probably arose because ostrich chicks will flatten themselves against the ground when danger threatens and escape because their plumage matches the ground.

If cornered, the big ratite birds fight out, kicking their powerful legs or jumping feet first at their enemy. The claw on the larger of the ostriches' two toes and the claws on the others' three toes are so strong that they can gash and tear a lion or a man.

When breeding time is near, the males of the big ratites send booming calls echoing over the countryside. The calls sound rather like a lion's roar, but they attract the females. The male takes a harem of several females and scrapes a hole in the ground in which the females lay their eggs. As many as 120 rhea eggs

have been found in one nest, but usually a ratite bird's nest contains ten to 40 eggs. The male birds usually raise the chicks.

Ratite eggs are huge. An ostrich egg – the world's largest – weighs three pounds (1.4 kilograms). It is white, almost round, and as big as a baby's head. One scrambled ostrich egg is enough to feed a dozen people. The eggs of emus and cassowaries are dark green, and each egg is equal to a dozen chicken eggs in content. The rhea's egg is slightly smaller and greenish tan in colour.

The fifth family of ratite birds is made up of the three species of kiwis. These birds live only in New Zealand. They are much smaller than the other ratite birds, being the size of large chickens. The three species – the brown kiwi, the great spotted kiwi and little spotted kiwi, both of the South Island, are very similar. Their feathers look much like hair. They have no tails and their wings are only two inches (five centimetres) long and hidden under the body feathers. Unlike all other birds, their nostrils are at the tips of their long bills. They probably smell their way around as they hunt at night and in any case cannot see well. They spend the day in their burrows.

All the ratite birds were more plentiful in the past than they are today because they have been hunted by man. Ostriches have been killed for their plumes, and rhea feathers used to make feather dusters. All the birds have been hunted for their meat, and the emu has been slaughtered because it damages crops. The kiwi is now a rare bird because much of the forest in which it lives has been cleared, and animals introduced into New Zealand have killed kiwis.

Owls

World-wide land birds, owls are divided into two families: the barn owls with ten species and the typical owls with 120 species. There are similarities between the two groups, but also several differences. Barn owls have heart-shaped faces with small eyes and rather long, hooked beaks. Typical owls have very large eyes set in round faces and short, hooked beaks. Barn owls have longish legs with feathered bare toes. One toe of each foot is a claw with a toothed comb, which the barn owl uses to preen its feathers. Typical owls have short legs and the toes are feathered.

Barn owls are from 13 to 18 inches (33 to 46 centimetres) long whereas typical owls are from five and a quarter to 27 inches (13 to 79 centimetres) long. All female owls are slightly longer than their mates. All owls eat and hunt in the same way, and most of them hunt by night. They catch small mammals, birds, reptiles, amphibians, fish, crabs and insects. They use their excellent powers of hearing as well as their good sight to locate their prey. Then the owl swoops down swiftly and silently to grab the creature in its claws. It swallows its prey whole, later coughing out neat little balls, called pellets, of fur, bone, feathers and other parts it cannot digest. These pellets are of interest to zoologists for locating animals on which owls prey.

In mild climates, barn owls have no regular breeding time. A pair, mated for life, raise their young when food is plentiful. Barn owls are found throughout the world, except in New Zealand. Only one barn owl is found in the New World, and this is the common barn owl. It is also found in Europe, Africa, India, south-eastern Asia and Australia.

Barn owls do not migrate, but several typical owls do. The snowy owl is a migrating typical owl. It nests on the ground in the Arctic tundra around the world, and winters as far south as the central United States, France, Germany, southern Russia, India and Japan. It

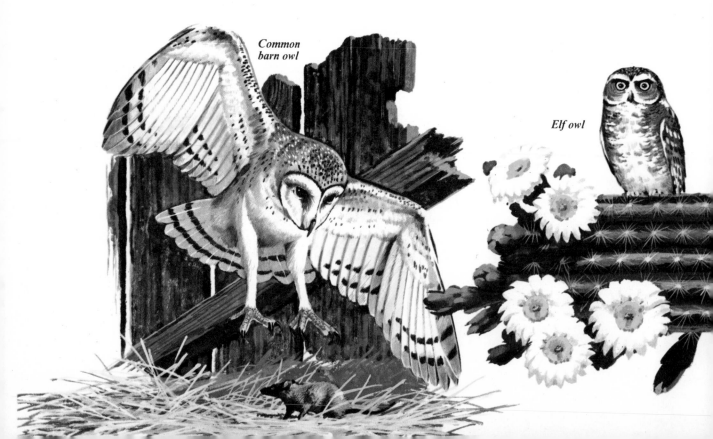

Common barn owl

Elf owl

Burrowing owl

Snowy owl

hunts by day, its white feathers camouflaging it against the snow. The snowy owl has feathers around its bill and feet to keep it warm. One of the first bird pictures ever drawn is of a pair of snowy owls with their chick. It is scratched on the wall of a cave in France by a Stone Age man.

Some typical owls are called horned owls because they have tufts of feathers on their heads that look just like horns. They include the great horned owl of the New World and the eagle owl of Europe and Asia. These birds are fierce owls, attacking such large animals as hares, geese and snakes. Another group of owls are the hawk owls, which get their name because they may hover, swoop and dive like hawks after their prey.

The most common owl in Britain is the tawny owl, whose eerie but musical hooting can often be heard at night. It is found in Europe, apart from Ireland, and in parts of Asia and North Africa. It is also known as the brown owl and wood owl. Tawny owls are reddish brown streaked with dark brown. They can also be grey, although the grey birds are rarely found in Britain.

A most unusual owl is the burrowing owl of the western United States and Central and South America. It digs a burrow in the ground or uses ·another animal's burrow in which to lay its eggs and to escape from danger. The young hiss like rattlesnakes to ward off enemies.

The smallest owl is not the little owl of Europe, Asia and North Africa, which is eight and a half inches (21 centimetres) long. It is the elf owl of the south-western United States and northern Mexico. It is only five and a quarter inches (13 centimetres) in length. It rests by day in a hole in a giant cactus and nests there too, raising three chicks a year on an insect diet. Elf owls also live in forests.

Oystercatchers

European oystercatcher

These shy wading birds are found on sea coasts and estuaries on all continents where the climate is mild, and on some inland waters of the Old World. Most notable in any of the six kinds of oystercatchers is the strong bill, which is twice as long as the bird's head. It uses its bill to catch oysters and other shellfish, small crabs, worms and insects. Oystercatchers use their bills like a chisel to pry clinging shells from rocks and as a probe to find food in the sand. It can also be used like a hammer to pound shellfish on the shore until the shells break, as a blade to twist open the shells, and as a pair of pincers to snatch out the juicy flesh inside.

Oystercatchers have black and white plumage or are black all over. The black birds are not found in Europe or Asia.

Male oystercatchers perform courtship dances with shrill piping calls. They compete with each other to attract the females. But the dance also serves to warn off other males from a male oystercatcher's territory. Three or four eggs are laid in a nest scraped out in grass, pebbles, mud or sand. The first egg may be left alone by the parents and is often lost to gulls.

Parrots

People who live in Europe, northern Asia and North America usually think of parrots as gaudy birds in a zoo or a cage. But in Australasia, Africa, South and Central America and southern Asia, parrots are heard and see in the wild as much as crows are in northern lands.

Most of the 315 species of the parrot family – which includes parakeets, cockatoos, macaws, lovebirds, lories, lorikeets and budgerigars as well as parrots – make good cage birds. Parakeets were kept as cage birds as long as 2500 years ago. Parrots have been kept ever since because of their bright colours, their longevity, and the way in which they use a foot to lift food to their mouths. The medium-sized parrots are very good talking birds and can imitate almost any sound. Although they seem to talk, parrots do not understand what they are saying. This is why learning to repeat something without understanding it is called 'learning parrot-fashion'.

Although all the various parrots differ widely in appearance, they all have strong, down-curved, hooked bills and feet with two claws in front and two behind. In the wild, flocks of parrots fly screeching through forests and over grasslands. They eat fruit, nuts, grain, leaves, flowers and nectar. Parrots can be helpful birds because they carry pollen as they feed, thus pollinating plants; they also eat harmful insects. But parrots also raid orchards and corn-fields. Some parrots take so much nectar that they fall to the ground in a stupor and do not recover for an hour or two.

The smallest parrots are the pygmy parrots of New Guinea, which are only three to four inches (eight to ten centimetres) long. They do not live long in captivity and so cannot be kept as pets. Another group of unusual parrots are the bat parrots or hanging parrots of south-eastern Asia. These parrots roost in groups, hanging upside-down like bats.

Central and South America is the home of the long-tailed, gaudy macaws, which are the largest parrots. The blue and yellow macaw is one of the most handsome macaws, and it is often seen in zoos. Also to be found in this region are the amazon parrots which, unlike macaws, are good talkers. The yellow-headed amazon is a favourite pet bird in America. It is 15 inches (38 centimetres) long.

Only 18 species of parrots live in Africa, and half of this number are love-

Blue and yellow macaw

Kaka

Rainbow lorikeet

Yellow-headed Amazon

birds. These small parrots get their name from their habit of nestling close to each other as they perch – a pair of lovebirds in a cage will sit for hours huddled together. Another parrot found only in Africa is the African grey parrot, perhaps the best mimic of all talking birds. Henry VIII owned an African grey parrot.

Australia, Malaysia and New Guinea are home to many different kinds of parrots. Lories and lorikeets are small to medium-sized parrots that fly in huge flocks. As many as a thousand rainbow lorikeets can be seen at one time, alighting together as they look for flowers to crush in their bills. Parakeets are small parrots of this region with long, pointed tails. The best known parakeet is the budgerigar, which is probably the most common of all Australian parrots. In the wild, budgerigars are mostly green with bands of yellow and black. They travel in flocks of thousands, feeding on the seeds of shrubs and grass and are never found far from water. Breeders have changed the colours of these popular talking pets by mating the odd-coloured birds that occasionally hatch out. The cockatoos are another group of parrots found in this region. They are large parrots with crests on their heads and powerful bills. The black cockatoo or palm cockatoo can crack nuts that a man would have to use a hammer or an axe to open.

Some of the strangest parrots are found in New Zealand. The kea is about the size of a crow. In the winter, the cold drives it to eat dead sheep and it may even attack live ones. It is the only parrot that eats meat. The kaka is about the same size as the kea. It once provided meat and feathered cloaks for the Maoris. Unlike the kea, the kaka is a protected bird.

Black cockatoo

Budgerigar

Kea

Indian peafowl ♂

Peacocks

One of the most thrilling sights in the world of birds is the display of the peacock. To attract the female, the male raises his train of shimmering blueish green feathers with their strange 'eyes' into a wonderful fan that frames his elegant, crested blue head. Although the peacock lives in the wild only in Asia, its magnificent display is known to many because peacocks have long been popular birds for adorning the gardens of palaces and rich homes and are kept in zoos around the world.

The peacock and the peahen are the names of the male and female peafowl, which belong to the pheasant family. They live in jungles and forests, roosting in the trees at night. They fly clumsily and make screeching calls. There are three species. The Indian peafowl or common peafowl of India and Sri Lanka (Ceylon) is the peafowl most often seen in zoos and gardens. The Javanese peafowl of south-eastern Asia is very similar, but has a green head and neck.

The third species is the Congo peacock, which is the only pheasant to be found in Africa. It lacks the train of the Asian peacocks, but spreads its wings and tail in display. The Congo peacock was unknown to naturalists until an American ornithologist, Dr James Chapin, found an unknown feather in the head-dress of a pygmy from the Congo. Two stuffed birds, wrongly identified, were then located in a museum in Belgium and Dr Chapin returned to the Congo and discovered live Congo peacocks in 1936.

Pelicans

'A wonderful bird is the pelican, His bill will hold more than his belly can.' This famous little rhyme is in fact true. The lower part of the pelican's bill has a leathery unfeathered pouch that can hold two or three times as much food as its stomach. The pouch is used as a net to capture fish, but the bird does not carry its catch in its pouch. As soon as it has caught a pouchful, the pelican tips its bill down to let the water run out, and then tips its head back and swallows the fish. The pelican also uses its bill as a feeding bowl for its chicks. After swallowing a catch, it returns to the nest and coughs the half-digested fish back into the pouch. The chicks are then fed or can put their heads into the pouch to help themselves. When the pelican is not using its pouch, the bird pulls it in flat against the bill. Pelicans rest with their bills pointing downwards and they fly with their necks drawn back. Both these positions tend to hide the bill so it is not easily seen.

Pelicans are sociable birds and like to be in each other's company. They fly, roost, feed and breed in dense colonies. In flight, pelicans follow each other in formations, strung out in a long line or a V-shape. Pelicans float well because they have hollow bones that weigh little. With their lungs, they can inflate air sacs that lie under their skin like tiny balloons. Pelicans fly strongly, but have difficulty getting into the air because they are so large. They have to land with their feet spread out like water skis to break their fall.

Pelicans live on sea shores and inland lakes in the warmer parts of the world. There are eight species altogether. They range in size from four to six feet (120 to 180 centimetres) and have wingspans of up to ten feet (three metres). The largest pelicans are three species of white pelicans. The eastern white pelican, which is also known just as the white pelican, lives in colonies scattered here and there in Africa, south-eastern Europe and southern Asia. The dalmatian pelican lives in south-eastern Europe and in central Asia as far east as China. The American white pelican is found only in the New World. These three birds are very similar in appearance, being all white except for a band of black on the wings, and having grey, yellow or orange bills. White pelicans often fish together in a group containing as many as a hundred birds. They form a half-circle facing the shore and then thrash their wings and splash the water as they move in towards the shore. The fish flee towards shallower water, but the pelicans follow, drawing in to form a circle. Soon the fish are trapped in the shallows by a circle of pelicans and easily scooped up in the birds' pouches.

The Australian pelican is one of the most attractive pelicans. It has a white body with black and white wings, grey legs and feet, and a pretty pink pouch beneath its fawn-coloured bill.

The brown pelican, which is smaller and darker in colour than the white pelicans, lives only in the New World. It is also different from the white pelicans because it dives into the water for fish instead of dipping its head down while floating on the surface.

Fossils of pelicans show that these birds have survived without changing for the last 35 million years. However, pelicans are now so much in danger that they are protected by law in many places.

Brown pelican

Eastern
white pelican

Penguins

King penguin

Adelie penguin

Most people in the northern hemisphere think of penguins as birds that live among the ice and snow of the coasts of Antarctica. This is true of the great emperor penguin, which stands four feet (120 centimetres) tall and weighs up to 100 pounds (45 kilograms), and of the smaller Adelie penguin, which is 30 inches (75 centimetres) tall. But many penguins live outside Antarctica, inhabiting islands and coasts washed by cold water currents that flow northward from Antarctic seas. One of these currents flows to the equator and there, on the Galapagos Islands off the coast of Ecuador, lives the Galapagos penguin. Penguins are also found in the cold waters that flow along the coasts of New Zealand, southern Australia, South Africa and southern South America.

Penguins lost the ability to fly millions of years ago. Their wings have turned into flat, strong flippers with which they paddle themselves through and under the water. Sometimes they swim like porpoises, going a little way under water and then leaping forward through the air. When they come ashore, some penguins can leap out of the water and land on a ledge ten feet (three metres) above the water.

Penguins have short legs and their feet grow far back on their bodies, forcing them to stand upright. The birds waddle about looking like old-fashioned gentlemen in black cut-away coats and white shirts. Their flippers hang at their sides and look more like human arms than bird wings. The rockhopper penguin of New Zealand, the Falkland Islands and other southern islands is the most awkward of the penguins on land. It hops instead of walking, and uses its bill and flippers to help it scramble up rocky cliffs. The emperor penguin and Adelie penguin can run slowly. If they want to hurry, they flop down on their bellies and row themselves rapidly over the ice – rather like a man on skis, but much faster.

The emperor penguin mates and breeds in the coldest months of the year in Antarctica, when the birds huddle together in large colonies for warmth. Each female lays a single egg and then goes back to sea to feed. The male is left to incubate the egg alone, holding it on top of his feet under a loose flap of warm fur to protect it from the deadly icy weather. For 64 days of the long, dark Antarctic winter, he goes without food until the egg hatches. He is then able to feed the chick on milk that forms in his crop during the long fast. But after a few days, the female returns to feed and look after the chick and the male can go off to eat. When the chick is ready to go to sea, the milder weather of the Antarctic summer has arrived. The king penguin, which lives on islands around the Antarctic Circle, has similar breeding habits, but the males and females take it in turns to incubate the eggs.

All penguins nest in colonies. All but the emperor and king penguins incubate their one or two eggs by sitting over them on nests made of grass, sticks or stones. The Adelie penguin can find only pebbles to build its nest. The little blue penguin of Australia and New Zealand makes its nest in burrows or rock crevices. Penguin colonies are very noisy. The birds bark, bray, trumpet and croak at one another and at any intruder. Penguins defend themselves and their young by hitting out with their flippers.

Emperor penguin

Rockhopper penguin

Manx shearwater

Leach's petrel

Petrels

Petrels, shearwaters and fulmars make up a family of 53 sea birds closely related to albatrosses. Also closely related are the family of 20 storm petrels, and the family of five diving petrels. These birds spend almost their entire lives riding on the wind over the sea with their long, slender wings. The shearwaters get their name from the way they swoop down into the watery valleys between the huge waves, skimming or 'shearing' the surface with their motionless wings. The petrels are named after St Peter. He is said to have walked on water and these birds run and hover over the surface with fluttering wings. The name fulmar comes from an old Norse name meaning 'foul gull', because of its unpleasant musty smell. Sailors call the giant fulmar or giant petrel 'stinker'!

The petrels and their relatives take food from the sea as they fly, or swim on the surface to feed, paddling with their webbed feet. They eat fish, squid, shell-fish and garbage thrown overboard from ships. Some petrels follow ships, though not as persistently as albatrosses. Giant petrels may come to land to feed, where they sometimes find dead seals and whales on which to feast. Unlike most other petrels, the diving petrels dive under the surface to catch their prey.

As well as using their food to help them grow and give them energy, petrels and their kin make some food into a musty-smelling, oily wax in their stomachs. This oil is shot out of the bird's mouth at an enemy, and is also used to preen the plumage. It is passed from one bird to another in courtship and fed to the chicks.

Although they wander over the world's oceans in search of food, in the spring all the petrels and their relatives come to land in the far north or south to breed. In the north, spring comes in May and in the south, in November. The birds form colonies that may number as many as a million birds. Fulmars nest in rocky ledges on cliffs hanging over the sea, but most shearwaters and petrels dig burrows on ocean islands. The storm petrels and diving petrels stay in their burrows by day and hunt only by night. Each pair of birds incubates a single, large

Fulmar

white egg for about two months. It is then two to four months before the young bird can fly.

The shearwaters are great travellers. The great shearwater breeds on the Tristan da Cunha Islands in the far south Atlantic and then migrates in a vast circle north to Labrador then across the Atlantic towards Europe and back – all between April and about October. The slender-billed or short-tailed shearwater migrates in a huge circle round the Pacific Ocean. It returns to its breeding grounds in southern Australia and Tasmania, taking in New Zealand, Japan, Alaska and the western United States on the way! Shearwaters instinctively seek out their breeding grounds from great distances. A Manx shearwater that bred in Britain was taken to Boston, U.S.A., and released. It flew the 3000 miles (5000 kilometres) back to its breeding ground in only 12 days. This shearwater and some other shearwaters and petrels are called muttonbirds in Australia and New Zealand. Although the birds do not taste like mutton, they have long been used as food and are still caught and sold for eating.

The giant petrel or giant fulmar is the largest bird of the family of petrels, shearwaters and fulmars. It has a wingspan of seven feet about two metres, and looks like a stout albatross. It lives in the oceans of the far south. The fulmar is a bird of northern seas, grey above and white below, and is 19 inches (47 centimetres) in length. It once supported an entire community of people on the islands of St Kilda off Scotland. The people ate fulmars and their eggs, burned fulmar oil and slept on and under fulmar feathers and down. The islands are now a wildlife refuge, and the numbers of fulmars are increasing.

Storm petrels and diving petrels are small sea birds, no more than ten inches (25 centimetres) long. Storm petrels get their name because they often appear at sea in stormy weather. One of the most common storm petrels is Leach's petrel. This bird breeds in northern oceans, and migrates as far south as South Africa.

Phalaropes

Grey phalarope (summer plumage) ♀

Red-necked phalarope ♀

Wilson's phalarope ♀

The three species of phalaropes are related to wading birds but their toes are partly webbed so that they can swim easily. They spin round in circles on the water, dipping their thin, straight bills to probe for food. But the most unusual thing about phalaropes is that the males behave like females and the females like males. The female is larger and has brighter coloured plumage. She takes the lead in courting and lets the male build the nest of grass and moss. He also has to incubate the eggs and raise the chicks.

The grey phalarope (which is also called the red phalarope because of its red summer plumage) and the red-necked phalarope breed in Arctic and sub-Arctic tundras. They migrate to spend the winter on warm oceans, mostly in the southern hemisphere. Wilson's phalarope breeds on the prairies of North America and winters on South American inland waters.

Pheasants

Although they look very different from one another, the peacock, the farmyard chicken, the quail, the partridge and the pheasant are all members of the same family of birds – the pheasants. There are 165 species all together, and they are all ground birds that scratch about with their claws. They probe the soil with their small bills for insects and worms, and they also eat grain, seeds, acorns, buds and berries. The feet are bare, and they have four toes. One of these toes is a hind toe, and above the hind toe most male pheasants have a spur that is used as a weapon.

There are three main groups of pheasants: the New World quails, the smaller Old World quails and the partridges, and the true pheasants. The first two groups consist of rather dull-coloured birds with short tails, whereas the male true pheasants have beautiful plumage and long elaborate tails.

Pheasants are rather heavy-looking birds with rounded wings. Although they are rarely seen in the air, they can fly strongly for short distances. The quail of Europe and Asia and a few other Old World quails are the only species that migrate. Most pheasants spend their lives

Bobwhite quail
♂

California quail
♂

Argus pheasant
♂

Ring-necked pheasant
♂

Golden pheasant
♂

Grey partridge
♂

wandering over the territory where they were hatched. They like to roost in trees at night, and take cover in brush and bushes during the day. All pheasants nest on the ground, except for the tragopans or horned pheasants of Asia.

The quails of the New World are brownish birds about the size of a small chicken. The bobwhite quail lives in the eastern and southern parts of North America, whereas the California quail is found in the western regions. Related birds live in Central and South America. Both of these species were introduced into New Zealand in the 1800s. The California quail survived and is now fairly common there, whereas the bobwhite quail did not multiply and is now rare in New Zealand. Groups of bobwhite quails roost on the ground at night, huddled together in small circles with their tails pointing inward and their heads out.

Old World quails and partridges tend to live in flocks, like the New World quails. The Old World quails are the smallest birds of the pheasant family, being up to nine inches (22 centimetres) long. Quails are sought after for their meat, and in the early 1900s millions of quails were caught as huge flocks migrated. Quails are now kept for their eggs as well as their meat. Partridges are also eagerly sought as game birds. The grey partridge of Europe and Asia has been introduced into North America for this purpose, where it is known as the Hungarian partridge.

The true pheasants are some of the most beautiful birds in the world. As with many other eye-catching birds, the males have the attractive plumage and the females are greyish brown birds.

The ring-necked pheasant and the common pheasant are the pheasants that are hunted for game. The ring-necked pheasant is so called because of the white ring around its neck. It originated in Asia, but has been introduced into many other parts of the world. The common pheasant is a similar bird, but lacks the white ring and has a dark neck. It originated in Europe, but has also been introduced elsewhere, including New Zealand and Hawaii. But the most common pheasant is the ordinary domestic chicken, all varieties of which are descended from the wild jungle fowl of India and south-eastern Asia.

Quails and partridges scrape a hollow in the ground amid thick brush as a nest. A male and female together raise 12 to 18 chicks, and the birds stay together in family groups. But the true pheasants have different breeding behaviour. The males court the females by spreading their long elaborate feathers and raising their crests in elegant poses. The Argus pheasant and the peacock face their females, raising their great colourful fans of feathers to frame their fine heads. The golden pheasant has a cape of golden feathers cascading around its neck. This bird looks most magnificent from the side. It seems to know this and poses with its side to the female.

Each male pheasant mates with a harem of two to five females and each female scrapes her own hollow nest amid long grass or shrubs. The female Argus pheasant and the peahen each raise only two chicks a year. Other kinds of pheasant hens raise six to 12 chicks, some as many as 20, in a brood.

See also CHICKENS; DOMESTIC BIRDS; FOWLS; PEACOCKS.

Jambu fruit dove

Mourning dove

Bleeding heart pigeon

Pigeons

We have two names for these gentle cooing birds: the Anglo-Saxon word 'dove' as well as the French word 'pigeon'. Many of these birds are called both pigeons and doves, but in general the larger birds are called pigeons and the smaller birds doves.

At least one of the 289 species of pigeons occurs in every part of the world where fruit, seeds, grains or acorns grow. Pigeons are mostly small to medium-sized birds, but some pigeons are the size of large chickens. These are the crowned pigeons of New Guinea, which are light blue with maroon breasts or wings. The crowned pigeons have beautiful crests of lacy feathers on their heads. But whatever their size, all pigeons have small heads set on short, thick necks. They can suck water up into their

White-crowned pigeon

Passenger pigeon

♂

throats without raising their heads from the water. No other bird, except the related sandgrouse, can do this. Other birds take water in their mouths and then tip back their heads to swallow it.

Another habit that makes pigeons different from all other birds is the way in which they feed their young. In the pigeon's crop, a cheesy curd forms from the lining of the crop. This curd is called 'pigeon milk'. The young birds thrust their heads into the parents' mouths to take the milk.

The most common pigeon is the rock pigeon or rock dove, which lives in the wild in Britain and Ireland, southern Europe, southern Asia, and Africa. All domestic pigeons are descended from rock pigeons. Many domestic pigeons have escaped and live in freedom in cities. In the wild, these pigeons breed on ledges and in holes in cliffs and gorges, but the city pigeon uses buildings.

Another common pigeon of Europe and Asia is the wood pigeon, which is blue-grey above with a pinkish mauve breast and a white neck patch. Wood pigeons are pests because they eat crops and many are shot for this reason and for food. In North and Central America, the most common wild pigeon is the mourning dove. It gets its name from its sad, mournful cooing.

The pigeons of the east are the most attractive pigeons. They include the bleeding heart pigeons of the Philippines, which are named after their bright red breast patches, and the fruit doves, such as the Jambu fruit dove of Malaysia which is as brightly coloured as a rainbow. The large blue crowned pigeons are also oriental birds, but the white crowned pigeon is an American bird of a different kind. It lives in the Florida Keys and the West Indies.

The passenger pigeon, though it is now extinct, showed man that he must conserve animals. In 1870, flocks of millions of passenger pigeons roamed North America. Then men began to shoot these pigeons for food and in 1899, less than 30 years later, the last passenger pigeon in the wild died. The very last died in a zoo in 1914.

Buff-breasted pitta

Garnet pitta

Yellow wagtail

Sprague's pipit

Pipits

The 48 species of pipits and wagtails are small slender birds that walk and run about the ground looking for insects. Pipits live all over the world. Wagtails are found in the Old World but only in Alaska in the New World. Pipits are brownish birds. They all look very much alike and resemble larks, which are also ground birds. The water pipit or rock pipit is found throughout the northern hemisphere. Sprague's pipit is the only completely American pipit.

Although it is difficult to identify pipits, wagtails give no problems. They are usually to be seen near streams, wagging their tails up and down as they walk or stand. The yellow wagtail is common throughout Europe and Asia. Other wagtails of these continents include the grey wagtail, which is very like the yellow wagtail except that it has a grey back, and the pied wagtail which is like the grey wagtail but white underneath instead of yellow.

Pittas

The 23 species of pittas live in Australia, southern and eastern Asia and Africa. They are plump, gaudy birds, feathered in a riot of colour. They are also called jewel thrushes, because they can be as vividly coloured as jewels. The garnet pitta is a deep crimson like the garnet stone. Pittas are not closely related to thrushes, and in fact look very different from them. They are strange-looking birds with very long legs and very short tails. They are from six to 11 inches (15 to 28 centimetres) long. Pittas live on shady forest floors, where they become difficult to spot in the dim light. If they are disturbed, pittas run away at great speed.

Pittas live on insects and other small animals. The buff-breasted pitta or noisy pitta of Australia picks up snails and hits them against a stone or a log to crack open the shells. It is one of the few birds that uses an object to help it feed.

Plovers

The 56 species of plovers, which include lapwings and dotterels, are related to the sandpipers and oystercatchers. Like their cousins, they wade on sandy beaches and mudflats, lake shores and marshes. But many plovers leave the water and live on land. They inhabit open pastures and gravelly waste land, eating insects, worms, snails, grubs, slugs, beetles, caterpillars, insect eggs and berries. Plovers are common all over the world and are six inches (15 to 40 centimetres) long.

Plovers can run swiftly on their three front toes. They have no hind toes, but only a small bump where the hind toe should be. Plovers nest on the bare ground and lay from two to five eggs. They are devoted parents. When an intruder approaches eggs or chicks, the adult bird on guard will make mock attacks by flying straight at the intruder to drive it away or the plover will try to draw the intruder's attention away from the nest. It flutters off in another direction with one wing hanging as if it is broken. It may even drag both wings or pretend it has a broken leg. A man or fox following what he thinks is a wounded bird is lured far from the nest and then the plover flies swiftly away, wheeling back to guard its young. Plovers are among the few birds that will risk their lives for the safety of their young by play-acting in this way.

The lapwing is a common plover of Europe and Asia. It breeds in the temperate regions of these continents and migrates south and west to milder climates in winter. Lapwings migrating westwards to Ireland, Spain and Portugal sometimes miss their wintering grounds. They fly on across the Atlantic until they reach the east coast of North America! The lapwing is a handsome bird with its dark breast band, elegant black crest and bronze-green back and wings. It is also called the peewit from the way it calls 'pee-wit' over and over. It nests in meadows and farmland.

The grey plover is a common plover that breeds on the Arctic tundra around the world. It migrates as far south as

Killdeer

Grey plover

Golden plover

Lapwing

Africa and the southern United States. In its breeding plumage, it has a line of white separating its black belly from its grey upper parts. In America, it is called the black-bellied plover. The golden plover is a similar bird that breeds in Iceland and northern Europe. Its upper parts are golden speckled with grey, camouflaging it among the moorland grass and scrub. The lesser golden plover is closely related to the golden plover. It is darker than the golden plover, and nests in the arctic parts of North America. Lesser golden plovers make fantastic trips over the ocean when they migrate. One group flies 2000 miles (3200 kilometres) non-stop across the Pacific Ocean from Alaska to Hawaii.

The most common plover in America is the killdeer. Like many plovers, it has rings of black and white around its neck. This bird does not kill deer as its name suggests but, like the peewit, it is named after its cry of 'kill-dee'.

The wrybill of New Zealand is the only bird to have a bill that bends to the side. It can reach around rocks for hidden insects with its strange crooked bill. Wrybills breed on the South Island and migrate to the North Island for the winter.

Ptarmigans

See Grouse

Puffins

See Auks

Quails

See Pheasants

Rails

The 132 species of rails include coots, moorhens, crakes and gallinules. They live in temperate and tropical regions all over the world. The water rail is found as far north as Iceland, where there are hot springs, although it normally inhabits the warmer parts of Europe and Asia. The Virginia rail breeds as far south as the straits of Magellan at the tip of South America, and is found throughout the rest of the New World.

Most rails live among reed-beds on lakes and marshes. They are fairly small birds, usually about a foot (30 centimetres) long. All rails have slim, narrow bodies, which enable them to slip between the reeds on their long legs and long toes without rustling a blade or leaf. They can move about while still remaining hidden. These habits make rails such as the sora rail and clapper rail of North America a special target for people who go shooting for sport. On salt-water marshes, the hunters usually wait until the rising tide floods the reed beds and forces the rails to fly. Rails are not strong fliers and can easily be shot in flight.

Most birds of the rail family breed on or near water. They make simple grass or reed nests just above the water on clumps of marsh grass or floating plants. Sometimes they build on the wet swampy ground. Most rails take only one mate and raise two broods of from six to 16 chicks each year. The young leave the nest right after hatching, but are guarded and cared for by their parents. Often the young of the earlier brood help to care for the chicks of the second brood.

One of the best known rails is the coot. It breeds throughout Europe and

Sora rail

Clapper rail

American coot

92

Asia, often hiding its floating nest in thick rushes or reeds. The American coot is very similar to the coot of the Old World in appearance. Coots are able to swim well because each toe has flaps of skin that open out as the foot is thrust through the water. As each foot is brought back again, the flaps close. There are several different kinds of coots. Bonaparte's horned coot lives on mountain lakes high up in the Andes mountains in South America. As few plants grow there, the mated pair of coots carry pebbles a little larger than walnuts in their bills to shallow water or to a protected spot on the shore. There they build a mound of pebbles and lay their eggs on the mound.

Several kinds of rails are called gallinules, and the best known gallinule is the moorhen or common gallinule. The moorhen lives throughout the warm parts of the world, but not in Australia and New Zealand. The similar dusky moorhen is found in Australia. Gallinules have long toes to spread their weight and enable them to walk about on the water plants where they live. The purple gallinule of the New World is a gaudy bird, with its red bill, bright purple head and underparts and greenish brown wings.

The corn crake that breeds in Europe and Asia and winters in Africa is not a marsh bird; it lives among corn fields. Like all rails, the corn crake travels at night. Although they are not strong fliers, rails can migrate long distances. Many rails that have settled on remote islands have lost the ability to fly. One of these is the notornis or takahe, a 24 inch (60 centimetre) gallinule of New Zealand. It was thought that this bird became extinct in 1898, but in 1948 it was rediscovered in some wild valleys amid the Murchison mountains on the South Island. Under protection by the New Zealand government, the notornis may survive and multiply.

Corn crake

Moorhen

Ratites

*See Ostriches and
Other Ratite Birds*

Ravens

See Crows

Rheas

*See Ostriches and
Other Ratite Birds*

Roadrunners

See Cuckoos

Robins

The robin is a welcome visitor to the homes and gardens in Europe. It is a most attractive bird with its red breast, and it likes human company, swooping down to take worms turned up as people dig in their gardens. But the robin is not friendly to other robins, and each home and garden is often the 'territory' of one cock robin and no other. Should another cock robin come near, it is usually fiercely attacked.

The European robin is a member of the thrush family and is five and a half inches (14 centimetres) long. The robin of North America is a similar bird but is twice this size and coloured red from its throat down to its legs. American robins also live near people.

Other kinds of birds are called robins. In Australia, the name robin is used for some kinds of flycatchers (see FLY-CATCHERS).

European robin

American robin

Rollers

The rollers get their name from the way in which they perform rolls and other aerial acrobatics in their courting displays. Rollers are about the same size as crows and live in the warm regions of the Old World. The lilac-breasted roller of Africa is a fine-looking bird. It is chestnut brown above, with a bright lilac breast and a large blue forked tail. Rollers eat insects, lizards, frogs and mice. They spend most of the day perched on a branch waiting for insects or other prey to come along. Then they dart out or swoop swiftly down to feed.

Lilac-breasted roller

Ruffs

♂

Ruff

Like the rollers, the ruff gets its name from its courting behaviour. At breeding time the male grows a beautiful set of colourful plumes around its neck. The plumes form ruffs like those worn by Tudor gentlemen. The colour of the ruff varies from white through buff and orange to brown and black and no two ruffs are exactly the same. To court the females, which are called reeves, the ruffs gather in groups at their courting grounds or leks, which are usually situated on grassy hillocks. Each ruff occupies a territory two to three feet (60 to 90 centimetres) across, and may have to fight to keep it. The females gather to watch the courting displays and choose their mates. After mating, the reeves nest and raise the chicks alone. Ruffs breed in northern Europe and Asia. They belong to the family of sandpipers and snipes.

Sandpipers

See Snipes

Screamers

These three South American birds are rather strange birds. They get their name from their harsh screaming calls, which they give to raise the alarm when danger threatens. Hunters dislike screamers because other birds take flight at their call. But hunters take care to keep clear of screamers, for they have two sharp spurs on each wing that can inflict a nasty wound. Although they look unusual, screamers are wildfowl.

Screamers are wading birds, living in marshes and flooded forests. They have hollow bones and air sacs under the skin that enable them to float easily. Screamers are the size of small turkeys, and usually

Horned screamer

feed on water plants. The horned screamer has an unusual curved spike jutting from its head out over its bill.

Secretary Birds

Secretary bird may seem an odd name for this elegant bird of prey. But it was named long ago when secretaries and clerks used to keep quill pens behind their ears. The secretary bird's crest of feathers reminded naturalists of this habit. The secretary bird lives on the plains of Africa. It preys on snakes and other reptiles, rats and small mammals, insects and young birds. Unlike all other birds of prey, it does not hunt from the air but runs after its victims. The secretary bird is so unusual that it is placed in a family of its own.

Secretary bird

Shearwaters

See Petrels

Shrikes

Shrikes are fairly small perching birds that hunt like hawks but kill with their beaks instead of their claws. They prey on insects, small birds, frogs, lizards, mice and other small rodents. They often hang their catch on a thorn or on some barbed wire when prey is plentiful and return if food gets scarce. Because they hang their meat as a butcher does, shrikes are sometimes called 'butcher birds'. However, some shrikes seem to kill more prey than they need, just for the sake of killing. If food gets scarce, they often move on to warmer regions.

The northern shrike or great grey shrike breeds in northern Europe and Siberia and in Alaska and northern Canada. A bold, aggressive bird, it is one of the fiercest shrikes. It builds a bulky nest in a tree each spring, in which the female lays four to six grey eggs. The loggerhead shrike of North and Central America is a similar grey and black bird. It often searches for prey while perched on a telephone wire.

Most of the 74 shrikes live in the Old World and many are highly coloured birds – particularly the bush shrikes of Africa. The gorgeous bush shrike of southern Africa lives up to its name, being as vivid as a bauble on a Christmas tree. But it is very shy and rarely seen.

The name shrike originated in the same way as the word shriek, but shrikes do often sing tunefully.

Northern shrike

Loggerhead shrike

Gorgeous bush shrike
♂

Black skimmer

Skimmers

A skimmer's bill looks rather like a pair of embroidery scissors, three and a half to four inches (nine to ten centimetres) long, with a shortened top blade. The skimmer is the only bird that has the top part of its bill shorter than the bottom part. Skimmers fly just above the water of coasts, estuaries, lakes and rivers with the bottom blade cutting through the surface. When they strike a small fish or shrimp, the top blade clamps down. The skimmer has strong neck muscles which enable it to jerk its catch from the water and swallow it without missing a wing beat. The long wings beat slowly well above the bird's body and never touch the water. Skimmers feed mainly at dawn and dusk and may forage all night. They have eyes with pupils that open wide at night but close to a slit during the bright light of day. No other bird has these cat-like eyes. During the day, skimmers sit and doze in flocks on shores and banks, waiting for the dusk.

There are three species of skimmers. The black skimmer lives in the New World, the African skimmer throughout most of Africa, and the Indian skimmer from India to Burma and Indochina. The black skimmer is the largest skimmer, being 19 inches (48 centimetres) long. It has a red bill with a dark tip. The African skimmer has a yellow bill and the Indian skimmer's bill is orange.

When a male skimmer courts a female, he often walks in front of her with a stick in his bill. If the female grabs the stick, she accepts him as her mate. But if she pays no attention to the stick, the male knows he has been refused. Skimmers breed in colonies on sand bars in rivers and estuaries. Two to five eggs are laid on the sand and incubated by the female. The young are sand-coloured and difficult to spot.

The great skua is the only bird that nests both in the Arctic and the Antarctic. In the north, great skuas breed in Iceland, the Faroe Islands and Scotland. In the south they breed on the coast of Antarctica, the southern tip of South America, South Island of New Zealand and islands in the Antarctic Ocean. The three other skuas breed only in the Arctic. They are the Arctic skua, the pomarine skua and the long-tailed skua. Americans call these three birds jaegers. This comes from the German word *jäger*, meaning hunter. All skuas are hunters. They swoop down on small mammals – especially lemmings – large insects, fish, shellfish, young and old birds, birds' eggs and, when they find them, the bodies of dead animals. Skuas also obtain food by attacking flying gulls and terns and other birds and forcing them to drop a catch of fish. The skuas snatch it from the air as it falls. The great skua is the largest skua, being two feet (60 centimetres) long.

In Antarctica, the great skua nests near Adelie penguin colonies and feeds on penguin eggs and chicks. In the Arctic, it mainly eats fish. A single egg is usually laid in the Antarctic, whereas all the northern skuas lay two eggs. They return to the same nesting ground every year.

Arctic skuas place their nests close together in large colonies. Long-tailed skuas nest at some distance from one another in small colonies. Pomarine skuas scatter far apart to nest over the swampy tundra. All skua nests are rounded hollows in the ground. Skuas are fierce defenders of their nests and young. They will 'dive bomb' approaching animals and men, turning at the last moment and often striking the enemy's head with their feet. After the breeding season, the skuas disperse to spend the winter wandering over the oceans.

Long-tailed skua

Great skua

Snipes

Turnstone

The 70 species of wading birds that make up the family of snipes and sandpipers have many different names. But all of them walk or wade on long legs and have long, slender bills, either straight or down-curved. Snipes and sandpipers come in many sizes from the six-inch (15-centimetre) least sandpiper of America to the 25-inch (62-centimetre) curlew of the Old World.

Most of the snipe family breed in the northern hemisphere. Many nest on Arctic coasts and islands, and then migrate great distances to winter in the southern hemisphere. Thus snipes and sandpipers can be seen throughout the world, wading at sea shores and estuaries and on inland lakes and marshes, though some have left the water to live in woods and grasslands.

One group of snipes and sandpipers consists of fairly large birds with long bills. It includes the curlew, which breeds across northern Europe and Asia. The curlew likes crabs and also shellfish, which it has to swallow whole without opening the shells. The whimbrel is a similar but smaller bird of both the Old World and the New World. The marbled godwit is one of four species of godwits, which have very long bills. It breeds in North America. The willet is a large wader of American marshlands which shows a striking white band when its wings are stretched in flight. Several of the large snipes have names that refer to the colour of their legs, such as redshank, greenshank and yellowlegs. Many forms of snipe are hunted for their delicate flavour. So many Eskimo curlews were killed in America a century ago that the bird was thought to be extinct. But a few

Whimbrel

Marbled godwit

Willet

Eskimo curlews were recently spotted so it has just survived.

Another group of snipes is made up of small to medium-sized birds, being ten to 16 inches (25 to 40 centimetres) long. They include the common snipe. In spite of its name, this bird is rarely seen as it spends the day resting among marshes and the banks of lakes and streams. The common snipe breeds in North and South America, Europe, Asia and East Africa. If disturbed, it lets out a raucous call and flies into the air with a zig-zag motion. In the spring, these snipes make unusual display flights to attract a mate. They dive steeply towards the ground with their feathers spread out to produce a loud drumming or bleating noise. The long-billed dowitcher of America and the American woodcock are also medium-sized snipes. Like the very similar wood-cock of the Old World, the American woodcock lives among woodlands, where the colours of its plumage conceal it among the undergrowth. Woodcocks have been seen to carry their young between their legs as they fly, using their bills and tails to hold them tight.

The group of small snipes and sand-pipers includes the sanderling, which spends only six weeks breeding in the Arctic. In the winter, it is white with a silver-grey back and wings. In summer, it turns reddish brown. Several other snipes change colour with the season. The spoonbill sandpiper has an unusual spoon-shaped bill, but no one really knows why it has such a bill. The knot is another small wader. Knots were the favourite dish of King Canute, who may have given his name to the bird.

The turnstone is another bird usually included with the snipes and sandpipers, although some naturalists classify it with the plovers. It gets its name because it turns over stones to look for food.

The ruff is a snipe known for its un-usual courting behaviour (*see* RUFF).

American woodcock

Long-billed dowitcher

Common snipe

Sanderling

Sparrows

See Weaverbirds

Spoonbills

The bills of these large wading birds are like the flat wooden spoons that sometimes accompany tubs of ice cream. When it feeds, a spoonbill walks with its head and feet in the mud. It moves its half-open bill from side to side until it catches a little fish, a water insect, or a small shrimp or crab. Then it raises its head, closes its bill, and moves the top and bottom blades of the bill against one another as though chewing its food. With a final shake of its bill, the bird swallows its catch. Spoonbills feed at night in shallow salt-water bays and inlets at low tide. They rest during the day, standing in large flocks at the edge of the water.

There are six species of spoonbills in the world. The most striking is the only species that lives in the New World – the roseate spoonbill. This was once a common bird but, a century ago, men shot these spoonbills by the thousand to make fans from their beautiful feathers. In the United States, roseate spoonbills now survive only in a few small flocks in special parks and refuges, but larger numbers live in Central and South America.

The five other spoonbills are all more or less white in colour. The yellow-billed spoonbill of Australia has a bright yellow unfeathered face that matches its yellow bill and legs.

Roseate spoonbill

Indian hill mynah

Yellow-billed oxpecker

Common starling

Superb starling

Starlings

This family of 110 perching birds of the Old World wear silky dark feathers that gleam brightly in sunlight. Many are dark-coloured, but some have gaudy patterns of plumage. Some starlings of tropical Africa and Asia carry bright crests or wattles on their heads. Starlings are from seven to 17 inches (18 to 43 centimetres) long and are chunky birds that walk and run with a waddle on strong legs and feet. They can fly straight and fast, and many starlings migrate.

Starlings enjoy each other's company, flying, roosting, breeding and feeding in large flocks. They chitter chatter to one another, whistle and warble all day long and sometimes at night as well. Many starlings are such good mimics that they can copy the calls of other birds and fool naturalists into thinking that the other bird is nearby!

Starlings breed in many different ways. The common starling nests on ledges and in crevices of buildings in cities and takes over birdhouses in gardens. If they can find no other spot, they will use the ground and build large untidy homes.

Some starlings, such as the superb starling of Africa, build dome-shaped nests covered with thorny twigs and lined with feathers, hair or soft grass, and having a side entrance. Some species nest in holes in trees, some in holes in earth banks, some – in Africa – in holes in termite nests, some in rock crevices and some on cliff ledges. Some use the discarded nests of other birds.

Some starlings raise as many as three broods of chicks a year. Usually, each brood consists of four or five chicks. The female incubates the eggs, sometimes helped by the male. The males always help to feed the chicks. Starlings feed their young on insects, which are the most important part of a starling's diet. Starlings can help man by eating insect pests. The rosy starling of south-east Europe and south-west Asia follows swarms of locusts. It is a rosy pink bird with a black head, wings and tail. Starlings also eat fruit, grain, birds' eggs, shellfish, lizards, and bread and other table scraps.

The common starling is well-known

throughout most of the world's cities. Great flocks of starlings come to spend winter in the cities, roosting at night on buildings and in trees. They spoil the buildings and damage the trees with their droppings. Common starlings originated in Europe and Asia, where they can be useful as they eat insect pests. Settlers therefore took some of these starlings with them to other lands. But the starlings multiplied so rapidly that great flocks of starlings soon spread over the land and ate grain and fruit and other crops. In North America, the many millions of common starlings there are all descended from 100 birds released in Central Park in New York in 1890 and 1891! Instead of eating pests, they have become serious pests themselves, not only in North America, but also in Australia, New Zealand, South Africa and many ocean islands. The only parts of the world that common starlings have not successfully invaded are South America and Hawaii.

In the autumn, the common starling grows white tips to its feathers so that it appears to be spangled with white. These tips wear away during the winter, and in the spring and summer it has glossy black plumage. When the feathers catch the sun, they glisten green and purple.

Another well-known starling that has moved around the world far from its original home is the Indian hill mynah. But no one regrets the arrival of this bird, for it is one of the best talking birds. When kept in captivity, this mynah bird can learn to speak all kinds of phrases and rhymes, pronouncing the words with amazing accuracy. Outside their natural home, which extends from India to Malaysia, most Indian hill mynahs are raised in captivity. These birds normally live in the forests, flying around the trees in large flocks. They lay two or three eggs in holes high in dead trees that are too rotten for people to climb. If it can find no natural hole, the bird digs one with its stout bill.

The red-billed oxpecker and the yellow-billed oxpecker are two African starlings. They get their strange name because they ride on the backs of oxen, rhinoceroses, giraffes and other large animals. They eat the ticks that infest the backs of the mammals. The oxpecker can also give its host warning of danger, and the bird and the large animal live happily together.

Storks

Every spring the white stork returns from Africa and India to northern and eastern Europe. Faithfully, for 20 years or more, each pair goes to its own old nest on the roof of a building. The male and female work together to repair the nest, adding new sticks, branches, mud, grass, moss, rags, paper and feathers. They raise three to five young storks. The family stays until autumn, when it is time to migrate again.

The Danes, Dutch, Germans and people of eastern Europe look on the white stork as an example of happy family life. In folk lore, the stork is said to drop new babies down the chimney. In these countries, white storks are loved and protected. Elsewhere, they are not so

Wood stork

Marabou stork

Saddlebill stork

lucky and are rare birds. The white stork breeds from western Europe eastward across Asia, as does the black stork. The white stork has a red bill and legs, and is all white except for its black wings. It is a large bird, being 40 inches (100 centimetres) long. The black stork is similar, but has black plumage with some white underneath. Unlike the white stork, it lives far from man and hides away amid forests, often around lakes and marshes surrounded by trees. The black stork is a shy bird and seldom to be seen.

There are 17 species of storks altogether. Storks are found in all continents, but not in New Zealand, the Pacific islands, or northern North America. The only stork found in North America is the black and white wood stork. It breeds in the swamps of the south-eastern United States and in Central and South America.

The largest stork is the strange-looking Marabou stork or adjutant stork of tropical Africa. It is five feet (150 centimetres) long and carries a long pouch covered with bare pink skin. The pouch hangs from the stork's throat and is probably connected with its breathing. The marabou stork competes with vultures for carrion, eating any dead creature it can get to. Nearly as tall is the saddlebill stork, which has a yellow 'saddle' across its bill just in front of the eyes. It is also found in tropical Africa.

The shoebill stork is an odd bird which belongs to a different family from the other storks. It gets its name because its bill is shaped like the front of a shoe. It is a shy blueish grey bird, and lives in eastern Africa.

Sunbirds

The sunbirds are the birds of the Old World that are most like the hummingbirds of the New World. Like hummingbirds, sunbirds are small birds that live in the tropics and feed on the nectar in plants. They can hover in front of the plants, as hummingbirds do, but sunbirds usually prefer to eat from a perch. They also hunt insects and spiders with their down-curved beaks. The male sunbirds glisten with colour as do male hummingbirds but, like their New World sisters, the females are drab. In spite of these resemblances, sunbirds and hummingbirds are not related to each other.

The regal sunbird, found in Central Africa, gleams with all the colours of the rainbow. The purple sunbird of south-east Asia and the golden-winged sunbird of East Africa are less gaudy but still very beautiful. Sunbirds build nests of hanging plant fibres and spiders' webs. These often look ragged and untidy, but are neatly lined inside with feathers. The nests look like hanging masses of dead vegetation and so escape notice.

Golden-winged sunbird

Regal sunbird

Swallows

These graceful birds spend most of their waking hours on the wing. All day long they fly about speedily, dashing to and fro in pursuit of insects. They fly with their mouths open and have bristles round their mouths to help gather in the insects. Swallows have long, pointed wings that carry them high in the air and on long migrations. There are 74 species of birds in the swallow family, which includes martins. Some birds are called swallows in one country and martins in another. Swallows and martins are fairly small birds, from four to nine inches (ten to 23 centimetres) long. They live throughout the world, except for the icy polar regions.

Many swallows and martins have forked tails. The common swallow's tail is deeply forked with long outer feathers. Swallow-tailed butterflies are named after this swallow, because the shape of their wings resemble its tail. The common swallow breeds throughout the northern hemisphere and migrates to the southern hemisphere for the winter.

House martin

Swallows have weak feet and, although they can perch, they find it difficult to walk and rarely land on the ground. They have a twittering song. Flocks of twittering swallows or martins can often be seen perched side by side along telephone wires. Many swallows also nest in colonies. Common swallows often build their mud nests on the rafters of buildings such as barns. These are therefore called barn swallows in America and some other countries. Another bird famed for its habit of nesting on buildings is the house martin. It builds its nest deep under the eaves of a house, where the roof joins the outside walls.

House martins breed in Europe and Asia. In North America, purple martins nest in gourds hung up for them by the Indians.

Some swallows and martins do not depend on man for their nest sites. They burrow into banks and cliffs. The sand martin makes tunnels into sandy banks through the northern hemisphere. The fairy martin of Australia builds a huge mud nest hanging on a cliff face. An Australian naturalist saw one male bird carry 1,300 pellets of mud to the female, who did the building.

It is easy to tell common swallows, house martins, sand martins – and

Purple martin
♂

common swifts apart, even though all have forked tails. The common swallow's tail is much more deeply forked than the tails of the other birds. These birds have similar short forked tails, but the house martin is blue-black above and completely white underneath. The sand martin is brown above and has a brown band across its white underparts. The common swift is dark all over except for its white throat.

Common swallow

Swans

See Wildfowl

Swifts

A bird that can fly at 100 miles (160 kilometres) an hour is well named 'swift'. One of the larger swifts, the eight-inch (20-centimetre) needle-tailed swift of Asia has reached this speed. Many of the 65 swifts can fly as fast as 70 miles (110 kilometres) an hour.

Swifts spend more time in the air than any other land birds. The common swift normally lands only to breed. It sleeps and preens its plumage in the air. Swifts cannot walk, hop or run, nor can they perch. When they do land, they cling to the walls of cliffs, caves, canyons, hollow trees and even chimneys. Most of them prop their short tails against the wall, letting their long wings hang down. The needle-tailed or spine-tailed swifts have tail feathers that end in needle-like points. As they cling to a hollow tree, the points stick in the wood and steady the birds.

Swifts have tiny bills, but can open their mouths wide to catch insects. When a swift hunts food to feed its chicks, it

Common swift

fills its mouth and cheeks. Swifts make nests by glueing plant material and feathers together with a sticky spit that comes from a gland in their throats. Some swifts make their nests entirely of this spit. The nests may be attached to a wall of a building or a hollow tree. The chimney swift of North America nests inside disused chimneys. The needle-tailed swifts, and the common swift of Europe, Asia and North Africa, are among the swifts that incubate the eggs by sitting on their nests. Other swifts hang from the wall over the eggs to incubate them. The swift chicks can cling to the nest or wall as soon as they hatch. But they do not leave the nest until they can fly well, after some four to six weeks. If the young swift falls from the wall before its wings are strong, it cannot get up from the ground.

All the swifts that breed in the northern hemisphere winter in the tropics. Swifts cannot live without insects, and so must leave their breeding grounds long before the first frost. Swifts that breed in the tropics do not migrate. These include the interesting and valuable cave swiftlets of south-east Asia. The edible swiftlet is not eaten, as its name suggests, but its nests are gathered from cave walls to make birds-nest soup.

See also SWALLOWS.

Edible swiftlet

Chimney swift

Tailor Birds

The tailor bird gets its name from the astonishing way in which it stitches leaves together to form a nest. It pecks little holes along the edges of the leaves, threads plant fibres through the holes and draws the leaves together. It makes several separate stitches, knotting the fibre each time to prevent it slipping through the hole. It sews up a pair of leaves on a stem or a single large leaf to form a long pouch. The tailor bird lines the pouch with grass, down and hairs to form a hanging nest.

Tailor birds belong to the warbler family. The nine species are all small birds, about four inches (ten centimetres) long, and live in Asia from India to the Philippines. They are often seen in gardens.

Indian tailor bird

Tanagers

Tanagers are grouped with their cousins, the cardinals and buntings, in one large family of perching birds. There are 525 species in this family, and nearly half of them are tanagers. Tanagers live in the New World. All but four of them breed

Scarlet tanager

♀

Scarlet tanager
♂

Western tanager
♂

in the tropics and stay near their breeding places. The other four birds breed in North America and migrate to the tropics for the winter. Among these four are the scarlet tanager and the western tanager. Tanagers are among the most gaudy of birds and sport a bewildering array of dazzling patterns. The males and the females dress alike, apart from the four North American species whose females wear dull colours.

Tanagers range in length from four to eight inches (ten to 20 centimetres). Some have soft plumage that looks like velvet, and some have plumage of changeable colours. Tanagers are kept as cage birds for their appearance rather than their song, which is not very musical.

Tanagers live among trees, where their vivid patterns are muted as they fly through the leafy branches. Their food is fruit, flowers and insects. They build cup-shaped nests in trees or bushes and some add roofs and side entrances. The females lay clutches of one to five eggs and incubate them for about two weeks. Both parents share in the task of feeding and raising the chicks. In the tropics, many tanagers raise two or three broods of chicks a year.

Some species of tanagers are called honeycreepers, because they like to feed on nectar. Their bills are longer and more slender than the short bills of most tanagers. Although they look like the Hawaiian honeycreepers, they are not closely related to them (*see* HONEYCREEPERS).

Terns

See Gulls

Song thrush

Thrushes

Thrushes live in almost every country in the world where insects creep and crawl and wild fruits grow. These birds are well loved for their beautiful song, with which they regale us as they perch in gardens, parks, orchards, pastures, woodlands, fields and along country road sides. Full of bubbling notes, thrushes sing melody upon melody without seeming to repeat themselves. Some thrushes, such as the nightingale of the Old World, sing day and night. Townsend's solitaire, an American thrush, sings all year long, warbling and trilling its ringing notes from treetop perches and from the air. Some thrushes sing so sweetly that people keep them in cages.

Together with babblers, flycatchers and warblers, thrushes form part of a huge family of 1200 species of birds. About a quarter of these birds are thrushes, and they range in size from four to 12 inches (ten to 30 centimetres). Thrushes live naturally everywhere except in New Zealand and ocean islands. But the song thrush's loud musical voice is so loved by Europeans that they have taken this bird with them to New Zealand. It is now more plentiful there than many of New Zealand's own birds. The song thrush has also been carried to Australia, where it is as much at home as the scrub robin, one of Australia's own thrushes. The song thrush may some day be more plentiful there than the scrub robin, for the imported bird raises two or three broods of four or five young each year and the scrub robin raises only one chick a year. Thrushes have also been introduced into Hawaii, where the native thrushes became extinct around 1900.

In Europe, as in other continents,

Bluebird ♂

reddish in colour than other small brown birds.

Many small European thrushes are called chats, from the way they chatter rather than sing. They include the robin and the nightingale, although this songster can hardly be said to chatter. The common redstart is another chat. The male is a fine-looking bird with its chestnut breast and tail. The female looks rather like the nightingale. The bluethroat is an unusual thrush. The male has a blue patch on its chin and throat, in the middle of which is a red or white spot. Bluethroats live near water. Other chats include the stonechat and whinchat.

Asia has many fine thrushes, especially the white-rumped shama. This bird has a

thrushes come dressed in many different colours and patterns. The famous little robin with its red breast often lives near man (*see* ROBINS). Very different in appearance, but also a thrush, is the blackbird with its black feathers and bright yellow beak. Only the male blackbird is black; the female is dark brown. Like robins, blackbirds are fierce birds and will fight hard for food and territory. Different again is the song thrush with its spotted breast and olive brown back and wings. The song thrush often sings each note of its song twice, unlike the other European thrushes. The wheatear can be identified by the patch of white just above its tail. It lives in open country, unlike the nightingale, which prefers thickets. The nightingale is therefore rarely seen, but it can be identified by its plumage, which is over-all much more

Nightingale

Bluethroat ♂

Redstart ♂

white rump patch like the wheatear, but is otherwise very different with its glossy blue back and red breast. It is a very tuneful bird and is a popular cage bird in Europe and Asia. Many European thrushes are also found in Asia. Africa is the home of the white-starred bush robin, which is found on the slopes of Mount Kilimanjaro and in other parts of Africa. The bluethroat is also found in Africa, where it migrates during the winter.

The New World also has many thrushes. There are only a few species in North America, several of them resembling the song thrush. The American robin is twice as large as the robin of Europe and Asia, and its red breast extends down to its legs. The Eastern bluebird is a very pretty thrush. It looks rather like the European robin, but has a beautiful blue head, back and wings to contrast with its red breast. Central and South America

Blackbird ♂

Wheatear

114

White-rumped shama

♂

Whinchat

♂

Stonechat

♂

have a large number of thrushes of their own. The great thrush of tropical South America is one of the largest thrushes. One of the smallest and most unusual is the little wren-thrush of Central America. It lives in high mountain forests. Thrushes that live in the tropics do not migrate.

Thrushes feed on the ground where they hop, skip and jump about as robins do. They pick up beetles and other insects, worms, ants and snails from the ground and they also feed from plants, eating insects and small fruits. They do not catch insects on the wing, unlike their cousins the flycatchers. When they migrate and breed, thrushes often travel and feed in flocks. They build open cup-shaped nests of straw and plant stems cemented together with mud. Thrushes place their nests anywhere from ground level to the tops of high trees. Some will nest in tree holes or crevices in rocks or ruined buildings, and some will breed in bird boxes. Most female thrushes have to build the nest by themselves, but their mates help to raise the young.

Tinamous

There are 50 species of tinamous and they live in the forests and grasslands of Central and South America from Mexico to Argentina. They range in size from that of a small plump chicken to a plump goose. Tinamous look rather like partridges but are completely unrelated to them. Their closest cousins are the flightless ratite birds, such as the ostriches and rheas. Like these birds, they live, nest and feed on the ground, but tinamous can take to the air if necessary. However, they are poor fliers and find it difficult to avoid obstacles in the air. When in danger, tinamous crouch in the vegetation, hoping to conceal themselves. If the enemy approaches too close, they take to the air with a roar of wings and drop to the ground in the nearest patch of undergrowth that will hide them. Their flutelike voices often ring through the jungle.

Panamanians call the giant tinamou *perdiz de arca*. Translated into English, this means 'partridge of the ark'. The legend in Panama is that when the rainbow appeared over Noah's ark, its bright colours scared the giant tinamous so that the pair left the ark and hid in the forest, where they still hide. The eggs of tinamous gleam with almost all the colours of the rainbow. They are a shiny green, blue, yellow or purplish brown.

Tinamous raise from one to 12 chicks each year. In some species, the females go from nest to nest in groups, laying their eggs. The eggs are incubated by the male and he cares for the chicks. A day or two after the young hatch, he leads them to fruit, seeds and insects where they can feed themselves. Tinamous are delicious to eat. The pale green flesh turns white when cooked.

Giant tinamou

Little tinamou

Blue tit

Tits

These friendly and intelligent little birds live among trees and bushes in all continents except South America and Australia. Tits are also called titmice. This name has nothing to do with the little furry rodents called mice, but comes from two Anglo-Saxon words 'tit' and 'mase' meaning small bird. Tits are among the smallest perching birds. The smallest of the 59 species is the pygmy tit of Java, which is three inches (eight centimetres) long. Half of this length is tail. The largest tit is the sultan tit of eastern Asia, which is eight inches (20 centimetres) long. With its gleaming yellow crest and yellow breast, it is also the only tit to have really bright colours. Most tits are greyish or brownish birds which have bold markings.

The most common tits in Europe are the great tit and blue tit. They are also found in Asia and in North Africa. They can easily be recognized. The great tit, which is the largest European tit, has yellow underparts with a long black stripe down the middle. The blue tit has blue wings and a little blue cap on its head. Some North American tits are called chickadees from the sound of their calls. In Japan, the varied tit is a favourite cage bird and is kept in a special tall cage where it can exercise in its very individual way by turning backward somersaults. It can be taught many tricks and is a common street performer. The black tit of Africa is a blueish-black bird with only a little white on its wings.

Tits spend most of their days busily searching for insects and insect eggs on trees and bushes. They also eat small wild

Great tit

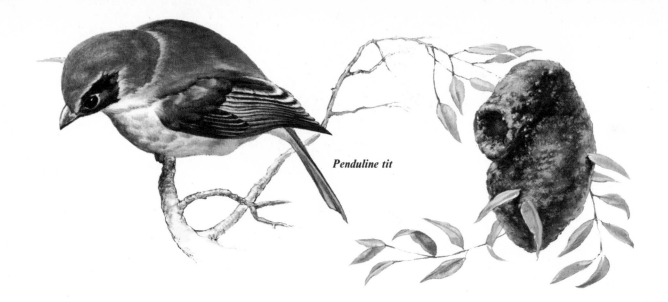

Penduline tit

fruits and can hang upside-down to eat the seeds of pine trees and other trees. Most tits do not really migrate, but wander in the same area all the year round. During the winter when insects are scarce, they are clever enough to find other kinds of food. They will come to bird tables to be fed, and like to be given seeds, pieces of suet and bits of apple. The food can be hung on the end of a piece of string. Some tits become so tame that they will take food from the hand. During the summer, tits may hide nuts, acorns and seeds for the winter. They hold a nut down with one foot and hit the shell with their strong cone-shaped bills until it cracks.

Most tits build nests in holes in trees, posts and rotting trunks, old woodpecker holes, rock cavities and bird boxes. Some tits chip out their own holes with their bills in rotting wood. The females usually build the nest. The material – grass, feathers, hair, moss, plant down, and mammal fur – is sometimes brought by the male birds. The tufted titmouse of the United States may pull a hair from a human head when it can't find hair elsewhere! The penduline tit of southern Europe and Asia is one of several tits that builds a hanging bag-like nest with an entrance shaped like a funnel at the top. Once inside, some African birds are thought to close the entrance.

The pair of mated tits raise broods of up to 14 chicks. The parents work hard to bring their young huge amounts of food. The great tit's chicks hatch just when leaf-eating caterpillars are most plentiful, so there is a good food supply.

Varied tit

Toucans

The huge bill of a toucan looks as if it is much too heavy for the bird to carry. But, being hollow, it weighs very little. Inside its mouth, a toucan has a long flat slender tongue with notched edges and a bristly tip. Toucans use their huge bills to pick fruit. In prickly places, they can reach into a thicket without putting their faces in the thorns. Toucans take fruit and water, as well as other birds' eggs and chicks, with the tips of their bills. Then they throw their heads back and the food and drink fall down into their throats. Toucans also eat all kinds of insects. The notched and bristly tongue probably helps in insect catching.

There are 37 kinds of toucans, and they live in the tropical parts of Central and South America. They follow each other as they fly weakly from tree to tree. They do not use their big beaks as weapons, but toucans have few enemies anyway. When they sleep, toucans lay their bright bills along their backs and cover them with their upturned tails.

Toucans nest in hollow trees and stumps and in old woodpecker holes. Their two to four white eggs hatch into naked chicks. For several months while their beaks and feathers grow, they sit on a growing pile of fruit pips that they and their parents spit out.

One of the smallest toucans is the 11 inch (28 centimetre) long blue-throated toucanet of Costa Rica and Panama. One of the largest, over 20 inches (51 centimetres) long, is Swainson's toucan which is found from northern South America north to Honduras. Toucans grunt but have no song.

Swainson's toucan

Blue-throated toucanet

Trogons

Quetzal ♂

Gartered trogon ♂

Trogons are fruit-eating birds of the tropics of Asia, Africa and America. They are famous for their bright gleaming plumage which, in the sun, makes them glitter and glisten with brilliant greens, reds and yellows. One of the smallest of the 35 species of trogons is the gartered trogon of Central and South America. It is nine and a half inches (24 centimetres) long.

One of the largest trogons is the quetzal of Central America. The male of this 14 inch (35 centimetre) long bird wears a magnificent train of four lacy green plumes that flow out over its tail.

The train adds another two feet (60 centimetres) to the length of the quetzal. It is such a splendid sight as it flies high through the rain forest that the ancient Aztecs and Mayas thought it was the god of the air.

Quetzals nest in holes in rotten trees high above the ground. They raise two broods of two to four chicks each spring. The female is plainer than the male and does not have a train. When the male incubates the eggs, his train hangs out of the nest hole, looking like a fern. Even so, the delicate feathers often get damaged at this time.

Turacos

Great blue turaco

The 20 species of turacos all live in Africa. They are also known as plantain eaters, because their food mostly consists of plantains and other fruits. They cry 'go away, go away' when a hunter approaches, warning other animals of the danger. From this call, they get their third name – the go-away birds.

Turacos live among trees, in which they are very much at home. They clamber up the trunks and run along the branches. The chicks crawl about the branches before they can fly. The largest turaco is the 30 inch (75 centimetre) long great blue turaco of Central and West Africa.

Turkeys

Columbus landed on America in 1492. On his fourth voyage to the New World, ten years later, the Indians brought him a gift of food which included turkeys. These were probably domesticated birds, for the Indians of Mexico first kept turkeys long before Europeans found the New World. The Spaniards took turkeys with them back to Spain and the birds rapidly spread over Europe. By 1577,

Common turkey

flocks of turkeys were common in English farmyards. The turkey got its name because people wrongly thought that it came from Turkey. They probably confused it with the guinea fowl, which came to Europe by way of Turkey.

There are two species of turkeys. The domestic turkey which is raised in millions all round the world for its meat is a variety of the common turkey. Common turkeys are found in the wild only in the United States and Mexico. They look very like domestic turkeys, except that they are usually less plump in shape.

Wild turkeys eat seeds, corn, nuts and berries. The turkey's gizzard contains pebbles and grit and the food is swallowed whole and crushed in the gizzard. This is the toothless bird's way of chewing.

The other species of turkey is the ocellated turkey of Central America. It lives in the jungle, whereas the common turkey prefers open woodland. It is about half the size of its cousin and has brighter plumage. 'Ocellated' means having eye-like spots, and the ocellated turkey has eyespots on its tail.

Vireos

Vireos are small perching birds of the New World. Vireos range from four to six inches (ten to 15 centimetres) in length. They are rather dull in colour, being mostly olive brown or grey. The brightest vireos have yellow throats or breasts. Many breed in North America and migrate to Central or South America or the West Indies for the winter. Vireos eat insects, seeds and berries. They hang their small cup or cone-shaped nests in the V of a forked branch. The nests are so well hidden among the leaves that the male birds can safely sing their sweet, warbling songs as they incubate the three to five eggs.

The red-eyed vireo breeds from Canada to Argentina. The northern birds and the southern birds both migrate to the Amazon for the winter. There they may mingle with red-eyed vireos that live in the tropics all the year round and do not migrate. The red-eyed vireo is a tireless songster and will sing ceaselessly through-

Solitary vireo

Red-eyed vireo

out the day, producing as many as a thousand songs every hour! It is called the 'preacher' because of its monotonous singing.

The solitary vireo is a vireo that is common in the temperate parts of North America. It winters in the southern United States and in Mexico.

Andean condor

King vulture

Turkey vulture

Vultures

Because of their ugly bare heads and their habit of eating dead meat rather than catching it alive, we look on vultures as rather unpleasant creatures. The remains of antelopes left by feasting lions, the bodies of cattle and sheep that die as they graze, animals killed by cars on the highways, and dead fish washed ashore are all food for vultures. We should not despise the vulture because of its preference for carrion; after all, we eat dead meat. Vultures help to clean the land of dead remains, and so are useful birds. They do not usually attack living creatures as the other birds of prey do, because their talons and beaks are too weak to kill animals and tear and lift their bodies. They must even wait to eat large corpses until the tough leathery hide rots and becomes easy to bite through. However, vultures may attack small, young animals.

Vultures can fly very strongly, and they spend hours soaring effortlessly far above the countryside. They watch the ground with eyes that can see eight times as sharply as our eyes can, and they also watch each other. When a vulture spots carrion, it sinks down and flies in a circle around the food. The other vultures see this flight, and come to feast from many miles around. Vultures cannot call to each other because they are almost voiceless and can produce little more than grunts.

There are two main groups of vultures: those that live in the New World and those that live in the Old World. Although all vultures resemble each other in appearance and in habits, the two groups belong to different families of birds. The New World vultures make up one family containing six species of these birds. The Old World vultures belong to the

Egyptian vulture

Bearded vulture

hawk family, together with the eagles, hawks and harriers.

Two New World vultures are the world's largest living birds. These are the Andean condor of the mountains of South America, and the Californian condor of California in the United States. They are four feet (120 centimetres) long and have a wingspan of ten feet (300 centimetres). The albatrosses have slightly longer wingspans, but they are much less bulky. These condors weigh up to 25 pounds (11 kilograms). The Californian condor is one of the world's rarest birds, and only about 40 of them exist. The Andean condor is also rare. These birds produce only one egg every year and the young do not breed until they are six years old, so the numbers of these birds cannot increase quickly.

The king vulture is the next largest New World vulture. It lives in South and Central America, and is famous for its brightly coloured head. The turkey vulture is the most common American vulture and is found throughout the New World. Both this bird and the black vulture are wrongly called buzzards from the way in which they soar. The sixth New World vulture is the yellow-headed vulture. It is thought to be able to smell its food, which is unusual for a bird.

Old World vultures live in southern Europe, southern Asia as far east as India and in Africa. The largest of them are almost the size of the condors. One of the smallest is the Egyptian vulture, which is 28 inches (71 centimetres) long.

The Old World vultures have different ways of feeding. This is useful, because as many as six different kinds may arrive at the same carcass. The griffon vulture, with its long bill and long bare neck, will poke into the remains to get at the soft intestines, whereas the strong-billed white-headed vulture will take the tough outer parts. The Egyptian vulture, with its narrow bill and feathered head, leaves the carcass alone and feeds off the scraps left lying around.

The Egyptian vulture is one of the few birds that can use a tool. It likes ostrich eggs but its bill is too weak to break open the large shells. The Egyptian vulture therefore picks up a heavy stone and drops it on the egg to shatter it. It will also pick up the egg and drop it on some stones instead. The bearded vulture or lammergeyer has a similar trick of dropping bones from a great height to crack them open. It can swallow small bones whole.

Wagtails
See Pipits

Warblers

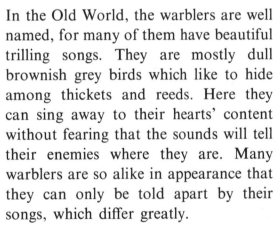

Reed warbler

Chiffchaff

In the Old World, the warblers are well named, for many of them have beautiful trilling songs. They are mostly dull brownish grey birds which like to hide among thickets and reeds. Here they can sing away to their hearts' content without fearing that the sounds will tell their enemies where they are. Many warblers are so alike in appearance that they can only be told apart by their songs, which differ greatly.

In the New World, the birds called warblers are badly named for they do not warble but mostly twitter. In fact, they belong to an entirely different family of birds from the Old World warblers. The New World warblers should really be called wood warblers because they are birds of woodlands. They got the name warbler because they reminded one of the first American naturalists of the warblers of the Old World.

The Old World warblers belong to one huge bird family together with thrushes, babblers and flycatchers. The warblers make up a third of the 1200 species in this family. They are small birds and are found throughout the continents of the Old World. Some of these warblers – the gnatcatchers and kinglets – live in the New World, but even so, they still belong to the Old World warblers. In the Old World, kinglets are called goldcrests (*see* GNATCATCHERS).

The warblers of Europe and Asia are almost all brownish birds. The garden warbler is a common warbler of gardens, parks and countryside where there is plenty of undergrowth in which it can lose itself. It is plain brown all over, and bird watchers can only recognize it by its lack of any special markings! The reed warbler is very similar, but has a light-coloured throat. It lives among dense reed beds on marshes, where it builds a deep tumbler-shaped nest. The great reed warbler is virtually identical, except that it is half as large again as the reed warbler. At seven and a half inches (19 centimetres), it is one of the largest Old World warblers. Much easier to recognize is the blackcap. The male has a black cap to his head, as the name suggests, but the female's cap is red. The chiffchaff is light green above and white below, like the willow warbler. But the willow warbler has a lovely warbling song, whereas the chiffchaff's song consists of two notes – like chiff-chaff – repeated over and over again.

In the grasslands of Africa are found the fantail warblers, which get their

Mrytle warbler

Yellow-breasted chat

name from their broad fan-shaped tails.

In Australia, New Zealand and the East Indies live the wren warblers, which are often just called wrens. They are not very small, but point their tails up in the air as wrens do. Many wren warblers are brightly coloured, unlike the other Old World warblers.

Most of the 113 species of New World warblers also differ from the Old World warblers in being brightly coloured, many patterned with yellow. The largest New World warbler is the yellow-breasted chat, which is seven and a half inches (19 centimetres) long. Unlike most other birds of this family, it sings well and mimics other birds with its strong voice. The myrtle warbler gets its name because it eats myrtle berries in the winter. An unusual New World warbler is Kirtland's warbler, which breeds in a small area of jack pine trees in central Michigan. It nests only among the new trees that grow up where there has been a forest fire. There are fewer than 1000 of these birds, and they migrate to the Bahama Islands.

Most warblers, whether Old World or New World, eat insects and turn to berries and seeds when insects are scarce in cold weather. Most of them migrate, flying by night. They cannot fly well in bad weather, and may be driven into buildings by high winds in the dark. Lights blind them and warblers crash into lighthouses and collide with each other in the bright beams. Many warblers are killed in these ways during migration.

Waterfowl

See Wildfowl

Waxwings

Waxwing

The three waxwings are birds that like each other's company. They always travel in flocks, keeping together even during the breeding season. Flocks of waxwings wander from place to place, seeking fruits and berries ripening on the trees. They also eat flowers and insects.

The best known waxwing is called the waxwing or the Bohemian waxwing. It breeds in the northern coniferous forests of Europe, Asia and America. It is the largest waxwing, being eight inches (20 centimetres) long. The other two species are similar but smaller. They are the cedar waxwing of the New World, and the Japanese waxwing of eastern Asia.

Weaverbirds

This family of 132 species contains many different birds. The common sparrows are weaverbirds, as are such extraordinary birds as the social weavers, queleas and widowbirds.

Weaverbirds live naturally in Europe, Asia and Africa, but house sparrows have been introduced successfully into almost every other part of the world. House sparrows like to live with man. They are adaptable birds, and quickly make a home for themselves and multiply wherever man should bring them. A few hundred pairs were released in a cemetery in New York in 1852. Today, millions of house sparrows live around the homes of North America.

Another common weaverbird is the tree sparrow of Europe and Asia, which also likes to live near man. It can be told apart from the house sparrow by its small black bib, black cheek patch and brown crown to its head. The male house sparrow has a large black bib, no cheek patch and a grey crown. The female house sparrow has no bib, whereas male and female tree sparrows look alike. Both kinds of sparrows are six inches (15 centimetres) long, and like other weaverbirds, they are seed eaters. They can be pests, feeding on crops such as rice. In Japan, tree sparrows are netted and sold for food.

Weaverbirds get their name from the complicated nests that many of them weave. The social weavers of southern Africa build the most amazing nests of any birds in the world. Social weavers look much like house sparrows and are about the same size. Yet they weave a nest that resembles a grass hut built in the middle of a tree. From 20 to 50 mated pairs of birds band together to weave a

Long-tailed widowbird

Tree sparrow

House sparrow

Cardinal quelea

Social weaver

Nest of social weaver

waterproof roof of straw. Each pair then builds its own little room, hanging it from the roof. Each nest has a separate entrance passage, and the whole structure may be 15 feet (four and a half metres) across and ten feet (three metres) high. The pairs of social weavers fly up the corridors leading to their nest chambers to tend their two to four chicks and feed them on grass seeds and insects. Village weavers are other African weaverbirds that may build hundreds of individual nests in a tree.

The baya weaverbird of India is trained to be a street performer. At its master's command, it picks up with its bill a bead in whatever colour a customer asks for. It can count from one to five.

The males of most species of weaverbirds wear brighter colours than the females during the breeding season. The male long-tailed widowbird of southern Central Africa grows a drooping tail over twice as long as his body. In dry weather, he can spread the tail like a fan, but in wet weather it can get so waterlogged that he cannot fly. The male cardinal quelea wears a crimson hood during the breeding season. This season varies from year to year depending on the arrival of the rainy season in southern Central Africa. It is then that the seeds needed to feed the young ripen. Pairs of cardinal queleas weave large dome-shaped nests of fine grass with a side entrance. The building takes a day and a half to make. The birds hang the nest close to the ground from plant stems and pull a leaf over it to form a roof. Outside the breeding season, queleas travel in enormous flocks over grasslands and cultivated fields. They eat the seeds and kernels of corn as they pass.

129

Canada goose

Nene

Black swan

Mute swan

Wildfowl

Wildfowl is a poor name for this group of birds because they are not fowls, like chickens or turkeys, and many of them have become domesticated. They are also known as waterfowl, which is more apt as they all live on water. The wildfowl consist of swans, geese and ducks, of which there are 145 species altogether, and the three screamers of South America (*see* SCREAMERS). Wildfowl live on rivers, lakes, estuaries and sea coasts throughout the world with the exception of Antarctica.

Wildfowl all have rather short legs set well back on their chunky bodies. Their front toes are webbed and they have broad bills. Many wildfowl have bills with edges like strainers. Mud and sand is sifted out of the birds' mouths, leaving worms and other small animals together with water plants, seeds and roots to be swallowed. Wildfowl swim well, using their feet as paddles, and most of them can dive either for food or

to escape their enemies. The northern-most species fly well and migrate long distances south to their wintering grounds. Some wildfowl fly well but do not migrate, and four species are flight-less. Wildfowl travel, feed and rest in groups. On migration and on food flights, they often fly in a V formation. Many species nest in colonies.

Although most wildfowl stay mated for life, their courtship is repeated every spring. Male and female swim towards each other, dipping their heads into the water as if they are bowing. All swans and geese, and most ducks, build their nests on the ground. They make bulky piles of grass, roots, sticks and odds and ends. Most nests are lined with soft down feathers that the female bird plucks from her own breast. A few ducks make their nests on rock ledges, in holes in the ground, in trees and in bird boxes. Wildfowl lay from three to 18 eggs. The

Mandarin duck ♂

Wood ducks ♀ ♂

female usually incubates the eggs, taking three weeks for the smaller ducks and up to six weeks for the swans. The downy young are soon ready to follow the female into the water.

The duck takes care of her ducklings without any help from her mate, the drake. The pen swan and her mate, the cob, take care of their cygnets together until they are able to fly. The goose and her mate, the gander, remain with their goslings in a family group until the next nesting season.

The largest and most graceful of the wildfowl are the eight swans. Five are white swans of the northern hemisphere. The other three swans are the black-necked swan and the small pink-billed white coruscuba swan of South America and the beautiful black swan of Australia with its jet black plumage and deep red bill. Black swans have been introduced into New Zealand.

Swans have necks that are longer than their bodies and they hold them in graceful curves. They glide over the surface of the water as smoothly as a yacht carried by a light wind. On land they tend to waddle, but still retain much of their dignity. The largest swan is the trumpeter swan of North America, which reaches a length of five feet (150 centimetres) and weighs up to 50 pounds (23 kilograms). The only other American swan is the more common whistling swan. It breeds at the edge of the Arctic Circle and winters south in the United States.

The remaining three swans live in Europe and Asia. The mute swan is not really mute but makes hissing and grunting noises. It has been taken all over the world to decorate lakes in parks and gardens and in some places it has escaped and gone wild. Although it is a beautiful bird, it is bad-tempered and should not be approached too closely,

131

Blue-winged teal ♂

Mallard ♂

Green-winged teal ♂

Shoveler ♂

Pintail ♂

especially during the nesting season. When mute swan chicks first fly any distance, they often do so above a flying parent. When they tire, they drop on to the parent bird's back for a ride. Bewick's swan and the whooper swan can be distinguished from the mute swan by their black and yellow bills. They breed in the Arctic and migrate south in October.

The 14 species of geese are smaller than the swans but they are still big birds. The largest are the Canada goose of North America, with its black head and neck and white cheek patch, and the grey-brown grey-lag goose of Europe and Asia. They are as long as three feet (90 centimetres) and weigh up to 18 pounds (eight kilograms). Some Canada geese breed in the wild in Britain and Sweden, but these are birds that have escaped from parks and turned wild. Domestic farmyard geese are descended

from the grey-lay goose, which is the commonest wild goose in Europe.

Related to the Canada goose is the barnacle goose, which breeds in the Arctic and migrates to Europe and some-times to North America. It is so called because of a curious myth that grew up in the Middle Ages, that said the geese hatched from barnacles. Although this is obviously absurd, the name stuck.

The nene (pronounced nay-nay) is a goose that lived originally on the dry mountains of Hawaii in summer, getting what water is needed by eating juicy plants. In winter it moved down to lower ground to breed. After settlers arrived in Hawaii, the nene was almost wiped out. The birds were shot and their nests and eggs destroyed by the pigs, rats and mongooses that the settlers brought with them. By 1950, only about 30 were left. Then conservationists began to make strenuous efforts to stop the nene dying

Lesser scaup ♂

Bufflehead ♂

Long-tailed duck
(winter plumage) ♂

Canvasback ♂

♂ King eider

out, and special sanctuaries were set up in several places to breed the birds. Now about 1,000 of the birds are living. A flock of them can be seen at the British Wildfowl Trust at Slimbridge, England. All the other kinds of wildfowl can be seen there too.

Most of the species of wildfowl consist of the smaller ducks. There are several different groups of ducks. One group is made up of the surface-feeding or dipping ducks. They feed in shallow water by suddenly up-ending their bodies and poking their bills down into the bottom of a lake, pond, river or marsh. These ducks are also found along sea coasts, and in estuaries, bays and lagoons. The male dipping duck is often gaily coloured, whereas his mate is a dull brown. The mallard is a common dipping duck found in the northern hemisphere around the world. The drake's gleaming green head makes it stand out among any group

of ducks. Most striking in appearance are the mandarin duck of Asia and the wood duck of America. These ducks nest in holes in trees, and will use bird boxes. Other dipping ducks include the pintail and shoveler of the northern hemisphere, the blue-winged teal and green-winged teal of America, and the shelduck of Europe and Asia.

Bay ducks dive from the surface and swim under water to feed, eating many small animals. They are heavy birds and must run along the water with wings flapping wildly to take off. The dipping ducks simply jump into the air to become airborne. Bay ducks include the canvasback and lesser scaup of America, which look rather like the pochard and scaup of Europe and Asia, the bufflehead of North America and the goldeneye of Europe and Asia.

Sea ducks prefer salt water and can dive deeply for molluscs on the sea bed.

They mostly breed on northern coasts and islands and migrate south. They include the various eider ducks, such as the king eider, which give us soft warm eiderdown for stuffing quilts. The long-tailed duck is called the oldsquaw in America. Mergansers are fish-eating ducks of the northern hemisphere. Mergansers have beaks with saw-tooth edges that help them grip the slippery fish.

Most ducks are found in the northern hemisphere, but some are found south of the equator. The muscovy duck, a valuable domestic duck, originates from South America. The Australian white-eye is a common duck in Australia. The Auckland Island teal has lost the power to fly, but swims around its home on islands near New Zealand.

See also DOMESTIC BIRDS.

Woodcocks

See Snipes

Woodpeckers

Throughout Europe, Asia, Africa and the Americas where the big trees grow, woodpeckers advertise themselves all the year round by their harsh calls and by the rat-a-tat-tat of their bills hitting wood. Bracing their stiff tails against the trunk for support, they use their strong slender heads and necks as hammers and their bills as chisels to carve nesting holes and roosting holes in trees and banks. They also bore into wood or soil for food, and even signal to each other by drumming on wood with their bills.

Woodpeckers have unusually long, sticky, hairy tongues with barbs on the tip. The bird can reach with its tongue into the hole it has drilled and rake out the grubs and larvae. Some woodpeckers bore into the ground in search of ants and other insects. Some American woodpeckers called sapsuckers drill into trees and drink the sap that runs out. They sometimes eat fruit as well. The acorn woodpecker of North and Central Ameri-

Green woodpecker

Wryneck

Crimson-backed woodpecker

Ivory-billed woodpecker

♂

Great spotted woodpecker

ca drills holes into tree trunks to store acorns for the winter. It makes a separate hole for each acorn, leaving the storehouse looking like a pegboard.

As a pair of woodpeckers chisel out their nesting hole, chips of wood fall to the bottom of the hole. It is on this pile of chips that the female lays her glossy round white eggs. Most woodpeckers lay four to six eggs and they are incubated for up to two weeks. They feed the young for three to five weeks.

The great spotted woodpecker is the most common woodpecker in Europe. It lives in all kinds of woodlands and in gardens and parks with many trees. It is one of several black and white woodpeckers with red heads. It is nine inches (23 centimetres) long, and is also found in Asia. The green woodpecker is another common woodpecker of the woodlands in Europe and Asia. The most striking woodpecker is the crimson-backed woodpecker of south-east Asia. It has a bright red crest, golden wings and a startling striped head. The two species of wrynecks are the most unusual of the 230 woodpeckers. They do not bore into trees, but use natural holes for nesting. One species of wryneck is found in Europe and Asia and migrates south for the winter. The other species live in Africa.

The smallest woodpeckers are the piculets of the tropics which are only four inches (ten centimetres) long. The largest are the 22-inch (56-centimetre) imperial woodpecker of Mexico and the 19-inch (48-centimetre) ivory-billed woodpecker of the south-east United States. But these large woodpeckers are dying out because the tall trees in which they nest are being cut down. It may even be that these fine birds are already extinct.

Another large American woodpecker, the 16½ inch (42 centimetre) pileated woodpecker has survived because it is willing to nest near the ground if it cannot find a tall tree. It resembles the ivory-billed woodpecker.

Wrens

Wren

The little wren that lives in most countries of the northern hemisphere is one of the smallest common birds, being only four inches (ten centimetres) long. It is the hero of an old story in which all the birds try to find out which of them can fly the highest. The wren stows away on the back of an eagle and when the eagle has flown as high as he can, the wren takes off and flies a little bit higher to win the contest!

The wren is the only member of its family to live in the Old World. All the other 59 species of wrens live in the New World. To distinguish it from the other wrens, the Americans call it the winter wren. All wrens are small brownish grey birds. They can easily be recognized by the way they hold their tails upright. They are loud but good singers. and usually live near the ground among bushes. They build large nests, often dome-shaped with a side entrance. The cactus wren of the deserts of the United States and Mexico builds its nest on a cactus or thorn bush. It is one of the largest wrens, being eight inches (20 centimetres) long.

The birds that Australians call wrens are a group of warblers (*see* WARBLERS).

Cactus wren

Yellowhammers

See Buntings

Index

owls, 72–3
oystercatchers, 74, 90

P

Pacific gull, 48
painted bunting, 19
paradise flycatchers, 41
parakeets, 74, 76
parrots, 74–6
partridges, 33, 42, 77, 84, 86
passenger pigeon, 88
peacocks, 33, 77, 84, 86
peewit, 90
Peking duck, 33
pelicans, 78
penduline tit, 118
penguins, 12, 80–1
peregrine falcon, 36
petrels, 82–3
phalaropes, 84
pheasants, 33, 42, 77, 84–6
piculets, 135
pied crow, 26
pied wagtail, 89
pigeons, 32–3, 87–8
pileated woodpecker, 135
pine grosbeak, 45
pintail duck, 133
pipits, 89
pittas, 89
plantain eaters, 121
plovers, 90–1, 101
pochard, 133
pomarine skua, 99
poor-will, 67
prairie chicken, 46
Prince Rudolph's blue bird of
    paradise, 16
ptarmigans, 46–7, 91
puffins, 91
purple gallinule, 93
purple heron, 52–4
purple martin, 107
purple sunbird, 106
pygmy cormorant, 23
pygmy falcon, 36
pygmy parrot, 75
pygmy tit, 117

Q

quails, 33, 84–6, 91
Queen Victoria's riflebird, 16
queleas, 128, 129
quetzal, 120

R

rails, 92–3
rainbow birds, 15
ratite birds, 70–1, 93, 116
ravens, 26, 27, 93
razorbill, 12
red-billed oxpecker, 104
red crossbill, 26
red-eyed vireo, 122
red grouse, 47
red-necked grebe, 44
red-necked phalarope, 84
red-plumed bird of paradise, 16
redshank, 100
red-tailed hawk, 51
red-winged Indian cuckoo, 29
reed bunting, 19
reed warbler, 126
reeve, 95
regal sunbird, 106
regent bowerbird, 18
rheas, 70–1, 93, 116
riflebirds, 16
ring-necked pheasant, 86
roadrunner, 29, 93
robins, 94, 113
rockhopper penguin, 80
rock nuthatches, 68
rock pigeon, 32–33, 88
rock ptarmigan, 46–7
rollers, 95
rook, 26, 27, 95
roseate spoonbill, 102
rose-breasted grosbeak, 45
rosy starling, 103
royal albatross, 10–11
ruby-throated hummingbird, 59,
    60
ruby topaz hummingbird, 59
ruff, 95, 101
ruffed grouse, 46
rufous hummingbird, 60

S

sacred bills, 61
saddle-bill stork, 105
sanderling, 101
sandgrouse, 88
sand martin, 107–8
sandpipers, 90, 95, 96, 100, 101
sapsucker, 134
sarus crane, 24
satin bowerbird, 18
scarlet honeyeaters, 56
scarlet ibis, 61
scarlet tanager, 111
scaup, 133
scissor-tailed flycatcher, 41
screamers, 96, 130
screaming cowbird, 24
scrub robin, 112
sea eagles, 35
secretary bird, 96
serpent eagle, 51
shags, 23
shearwaters, 82–3, 96
shelduck, 133
shoebill stork, 105
short-tailed albatross, 10
shoveler, 133
shrikes, 97
siskin, 38–9
sittellas, 68
skimmers, 98
skuas, 99
skylark, 64
slender-billed shearwater, 83
snake birds, 29
snipes, 100–1
snow bunting, 19
snowy egret, 54
snowy owl, 72–3
social weavers, 128, 128–9
solitaire, 31
solitary vireo, 122
song thrush, 112, 113, 114
sooty tern, 49
sora rail, 92
sparrow, 38, 102
sparrowhawk, 51
spoonbills, 61, 102
spoonbill sandpiper, 101
Sprague's pipit, 89
stage makers, 18
starlings, 103–4
stilts, 14
stonechat, 113